PDA*

*Personal Death Awareness

PRENTICE-HALL, INC., Englewood Cliffs, New Jersey

PDA*

J. William Worden, Ph.D.
and
William Proctor

*Personal Death Awareness

TO
ADW

COLLEAGUE–SCHOLAR–FRIEND

PDA*

*Personal Death Awareness
by William Worden, Ph.D., and William Proctor
Copyright © 1976 by J. William Worden, Ph.D., and William Proctor

Printed in the United States of America

Prentice-Hall International, Inc., London
Prentice-Hall of Australia, Pty. Ltd., Sydney
Prentice-Hall of Canada, Ltd., Toronto
Prentice-Hall of India Private Ltd., New Delhi
Prentice-Hall of Japan, Inc., Tokyo
Prentice-Hall of Southeast Asia Pte. Ltd., Singapore

10 9 8 7 6 5 4 3 2 1

Library of Congress Cataloging in Publication Data
Worden, James William.
      PDA—personal death awareness.

      Includes bibliographies and index.
      1. Death—Psychological aspects. 2. Awareness.
I. Proctor, William, joint author. II. Title.
III. Title: Personal death awareness.
BF789.D4W64   155.9'37   76-16188
ISBN 0-13-657213-8

PREFACE

After eight years as Research Director for Harvard's Omega Project, a study of terminal illness and suicide, I have come to the conclusion that many of life's problems, both emotional and practical, stem from an inability to confront the inevitability of one's own death. This book, with its primary theme of Personal Death Awareness, is my attempt to introduce you, the reader, to the freer, more meaningful life that is possible through a clearer understanding of your own mortality.

Because confronting your death can be, at least initially, a frightening and lonely experience, I have included numerous illustrations from the lives of patients with whom we have worked at the Massachusetts General Hospital. These individuals, whose identities are either disguised or presented as composites to protect confidential disclosures, should give you the comforting knowledge that others have trod the path that you and I must take one day.

The book contains a number of awareness exercises, many of which I use in teaching death awareness to medical students, psychiatric residents, and university students. They have found these exercises helpful and I think that you may also. Let me encourage you to use this book as a workbook in which to note your personal reflections and reactions as you think about these important issues.

In addition to the patients whose lives have touched and enriched my own, I would like to also thank my many colleagues on the Omega Project. Special appreciation must go to Avery D. Weisman, Principle Investigator of Project Omega, to Phillip Walsh, who served as research assistant in the preparation of this book, and to Joan Griffin who graciously typed the many revisions of the manuscript. My long-time friend William Proctor proved to be a congenial collaborator. Pat Worden provided helpful ideas and critical comments along the way. The Omega Project is funded by research grants from the National Institute of Mental Health and the National Cancer Institute.

J.W.W., Boston

We acknowledge with thanks
the following permissions:

"I Watched Myself Die"
by E. L. Huffine;
excerpts from article
in May 1964 issue of *Guideposts*.
Reprinted by permission
from *Guideposts* magazine,
copyright 1964 by Guideposts Associates Inc.,
Carmel, New York 10512.

"Cardiac Arrest Remembered"
by R. L. MacMillan, M.D.,
and K.W.G. Brown, M.D.,
from *Canadian Medical Assn. Journal*,
104:889, 1971.

"Dying in Academe"
by Nancy L. Caroline, M.D.,
from *The New Physician*,
21:11, 654-57, November 1972.

CONTENTS

There is only one liberty . . .
to come to terms
            with death.
After which,
        everything is possible.

Camus

I

Waking Up to Yourself

Chapter One

WHAT'S YOUR PDA?

A friend of mine was at a suburban party where one of the guests, a university professor, began to boast about his open-mindedness and willingness to confront any issue, no matter how distasteful.

"If we're going to solve the terrible problems around us," the professor said, "we have to be objective. I've learned to confront any tragedy—the war orphans in Indochina, a widow crying over her husband's dead body in the hospital, the racial hatred that some Americans have for others—and completely eliminate most feelings of emotion, such as fear or revulsion."

As he continued praising his own self-control, my friend, a committed enemy of inflated egos, began to sketch on a blank sheet of paper on a nearby desk. When a lull occurred in the conversation, he turned to the professor and said, "When you face tough problems, you really seem to have learned how to handle yourself."

The professor nodded smugly. "Yes, well, it has taken some work you know—a great deal of stringent, sometimes even painful personal discipline. And I do make wrong decisions sometimes, but not because I lose my head with any unnecessary anxiety or anger. It's a matter of knowing myself, as the Delphic Oracle advised."

My friend nodded solicitously. "Yes, well, how would you react if someone handed you a photograph that looked like this?" He pushed the paper on which he had been sketching toward the professor. A tombstone was clearly depicted and bore the professor's name, with the inscription, "1930-1976. May He Rest In Peace." From a mound of dirt in front of the marker rose a single flower.

The professor stared at the drawing for a few moments, gulped, and then began to stammer. He crumpled the paper in his fist, and his face flushed in anger. "I think this is thoroughly rude and not at all funny, if it's supposed to be a joke!" he almost shouted through clenched teeth. He stormed to the other side of the room to get himself another drink, and it took several minutes for the others to pacify him.

But my friend's point had been made rather dramatically: The professor may well have been open and detached about dealing with the tragedies of others. But when starkly confronted with his *own* death, he first froze and then lashed out defensively in an effort to avoid dealing with the issue.

Subconsciously, he had eliminated from consideration an entire dimension—perhaps the most important dimension—of his life. The shackles of fear and anxiety about his own limited life span prevented him from even *discussing* his own death, much less considering how understanding his mortality might enhance the quality of his present life.

This professor is like many whose fears of death have put padlocks of denial on important awareness. In the following pages, you'll be introduced to some keys that can help open these closed inner doors and free you to explore aspects of your personality and relationships that you may have avoided.

As a first step in helping you to break free from some of your own fears, take the following word association test. Words and phrases which we encounter every day have both a dictionary meaning and a personal meaning. The personal meanings are of special interest in understanding human behavior—your own behavior in this case. There are no right or wrong answers. Just put down the first word that comes to your mind.

BALL—	KEY—
CAR—	DEATH—
DOG—	FRIEND—
WOMAN—	HIGH—
BRICK—	TREE—
RED—	BIRD—
FATHER—	TIME

I am most interested in your personal response to the word *death*. After you read the word *death*, what was the first thing that came to your mind? I asked a number of people to give me their associations to death, and here are some of their responses:

death — life	*death — camp*
death — evil	*death — horrible*
death — sorrow	*death — grave*
death — black	*death — sadness*
death — destruction	*death — loss*
death — dying	*death — horror*
death — knell	*death —corpse*
death — tomb	*death — end*

Most of these responses have a negative connotation. How does your answer compare? Some people draw a mental blank when they see the word "death." They can't find an association, or they take a much longer time to respond to the word *death* than they do to more neutral words, like "ball" and "car." In other words, there is a tendency to develop what might be called a "death block." Many regard death as completely bad and evil, something which should be considered only if it's unavoidable.

Because of these negative associations, most people don't want to think about death, especially not their own. Their Personal Death Awareness or "PDA"—their sense of their own mortality— remains at a very low level. Perhaps this is true of you.

To test the level of your own Personal Death Awareness, try another simple exercise. In the space below, draw a line that you think best represents your total life span. The line can be any shape or length that you think is most appropriate.

Some people choose to draw a line from one end of the page to the other—in effect, a line without boundaries which ends only because the edge of the page forces the pencil to stop.

Others draw a line that curves back and forth. Some people find that they can't take their pencils off the paper because they don't want their lives to end, even symbolically:

Some draw a curved line with an apex at the top, indicating, perhaps, that the best portion of their lives is in the middle:

Those who have known hard times or frequent depressions may feel that birth and death are the least painful points in their existence. As a result, they draw an inverted curve:

Now draw another line of any length, this time a straight one with a beginning and an end.

Consider this line to be your total life span. Place a slash mark at any point along the line where you think you are today in your life's chronology. Now, complete the following sentences by filling in the blanks:

I expect to live until age _____

I am presently age _____

When you compare your present age with the age at which you expect to die, how much of your life do you find you've already lived? A third, a half, two-thirds, or more? Now look back at the line with the slash mark. How does your estimate of the time you have left to live on the life-span line compare with your numerical estimate?

Many people who have done this exercise have found that they placed the slash mark at an earlier age than their written guess. When you see your life starkly depicted on a line in front of you, like a racetrack or a road map, the tendency is to give yourself more time to live than you know you probably have.

How did it feel to commit yourself to a definite life span? Some people worry that they may jinx themselves by doing this. Old superstitions rise up and haunt them. Does this concern you? Did you feel any other discomfort? If not, what do you think made you feel relatively comfortable in doing this task? Take a minute and write down your responses below:

I was uncomfortable in estimating my remaining life span because _____

_____

_____

I was comfortable in estimating my remaining life span because _____

_____

_____

By this time you are probably experiencing an increase in your PDA, your Personal Death Awareness. PDA, by the way, does not refer to your awareness of death in general or of someone else's death, but to your awareness of your *own* death. It's a very personal concept.

I usually think of the PDA in terms of a four-point scale:

PERSONAL DEATH AWARENESS INDEX

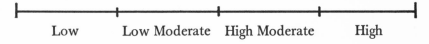

Low   Low Moderate   High Moderate   High

One of the most helpful ways to understand your PDA is to take a moment and recall the number of times today you've thought about your *own*—not someone else's—death or limited span of life. Maybe you thought about your age and evaluated your own progress toward certain life goals. Or perhaps you briefly experienced a fear of dying.

If such a thought didn't occur to you at all, then you're probably in the "low" range today on the index. If these ideas crossed your mind one, two, or three times, then you moved up through the "moderate" range. If you seriously pondered your own death or mortality four or more times, or find it a preoccupation, then you're likely in the "high" range.

Your Personal Death Awareness is a fluctuating phenomenon, moving up and down daily. Some days, you'll be more aware of your own limited life span, and other days you may act and think as though you're going to live forever. I experience these feelings, and I'm sure you do, too. Because you've been reading this chapter and doing some of these exercises, you probably have a higher PDA now than you did before you began reading.

Most of us usually register quite low on the awareness index because we tend to shy away from thoughts of our own death. Consciously or subconsciously, we deny that someday our lives must end. The more intense our denial, the lower our PDA.

When I first began working with the Omega Project, I was invited to a small dinner party at the home of some people I had just met. The hostess was a very efficient type who had planned everything perfectly in advance, from the hors d'oeuvres right down to the conversation. As if on cue, she said to me, "And what do you do at Harvard, Dr. Worden?"

"I'm researching death and dying," I replied.

She paled, looked very uncomfortable, and quickly focused her attention on another guest at the table. A discussion of death was definitely not what she wanted for herself or her party. I later learned that this woman was reacting, in part, to a series of recent deaths in her family. These losses had stimulated her PDA to an uncomfortable level; talking about death would have only added to her discomfort.

In addition, many families operate by an unwritten code that Personal Death Awareness must be kept at a low level, and so they avoid any conversation on the subject unless absolutely necessary. A woman said to me recently, "In our family we don't talk about religion, cancer, or death."

An elderly grandfather I know, who had been permanently crippled in an accident, dwelt constantly on his own death. "I don't know why God has kept me alive," he said. "I know I won't be here much longer, and that's the best thing because I'm no good to anybody."

"Don't talk like that, Granddad," his granddaughter replied. "You probably have years to live. You ought to concentrate on finding what God wants you to do rather than on giving up life too early!"

We assume the granddaughter was saying this out of love for the old man. Actually, it was to her advantage to speak this way in order to keep her own PDA at a manageable level.

One reason you tend to get upset when a major disaster occurs close to you is that it increases your Personal Death Awareness beyond an acceptable level. You identify with those who have died and become uncomfortable as you're reminded of your own mortality.

I was able to observe this phenomenon firsthand in Boston during the summer of 1973 when a Delta airliner crashed, immediately killing all but one passenger. Our hospital received the dead and injured. Because I was interested in how people cope with anxiety, I spoke with a number of the bystanders watching the incoming ambulances. "This really upsets me!" one woman said. "It's not just that so many people were killed, though I really think that's terrible, you understand. What really gets to me is that I could have been on that plane."

In other words, she was disturbed, not so much by the great loss of life, but by her own mortality. As the implications of death were brought home to her, she experienced a painful increase in her own Personal Death Awareness.

If she had witnessed this same scene on television, this woman might have conditioned herself to maintain a low PDA by ignoring or making impersonal the constant reports of deaths and disasters by the news media.

Doctors and nurses who work with dying patients also devise strategies to keep their own PDA below uncomfortable levels. They rely on in-house humor and often refer to patients as "cases" rather than as persons. In one New York hospital doctors sometimes refer jokingly to drug addicts and survivors of serious knife or gunshot wounds as "anti-death antibodies." Although most medical people are aware of the anxiety beneath their macabre humor, some are completely oblivious to it.

Some colleagues and I did a study of equivocal suicides. We found that the closer the deceased was in age, sex, and professional standing to the attending physician, the less chance there was that the death would be listed as a suicide in hospital records.

More likely, the report would say "accidental death." The doctor's identification with the deceased probably raised his own PDA, and prompted him to unconsciously decide in favor of an accident.

Awareness of death is always tempered by denial. Some denial of death is necessary and important, for without a degree of denial of your own death, you can't function effectively. As François, Duc de La Rochefoucauld said, "Neither the sun nor death can be looked at steadily."

Dr. Avery Weisman, my colleague on the Omega Project, said in a recent book, "The purpose of denial is not simply to avoid danger but to prevent loss of a significant relationship ... with someone essential to self-esteem. ... Denial helps to maintain a simplified yet constant relationship with significant others, especially at a moment of crisis."[1]

Despite attempts at denial, *some* awareness of your own mortality, however low, is always there in your consciousness. Are you aware of the pressure of the chair on your buttocks as you sit and read this book? Until I mentioned it, you were probably quite unaware of the pressure. But now that I have mentioned it, your awareness of it has increased. The pressure hasn't changed, of course. You may be squirming more now, but the pressure is the same as it was before.

Similarly, in this book I am encouraging you to consider a pressure which is already there—your own limited life span and the fact that someday you will indeed die. I am purposely asking you to raise your Personal Death Awareness so that you can begin to perceive an entire range of choices about your life and death that you might not have been aware of before.

In Gestalt psychotherapy, there's a technique called "experiencing polarities" which can help people understand themselves better and become more effective persons.[2] If you're very shy, for example, the therapist, through suggested experiments with other people, may help you experience extremely extroverted behavior—the opposite "pole" to your usual shyness. The purpose isn't to make you *become* an extrovert, but rather to give you some experience with a side of your personality you've never tested before. By acting out an extroverted role, you can increase your awareness of what it's like. Perhaps you can acquire enough flexibility so that you don't have to hover around your "shy" behavioral extreme just because it's familiar and safe.

Many people are afraid to try unfamiliar behavior extremes because they're afraid they may get stuck there. I've never known this to happen. More likely, they'll realize they can do and experience things they previously considered impossible.

Just as there are extremes of introversion and extroversion, there are extremes of Personal Death Awareness. You may have willingly experienced only one polarity—the low side of the awareness index. Any high death awareness you've experienced was probably associated with something very unpleasant, such as the death of a friend or loved one, and that makes you resist increasing your death awareness. But I've often found that if a person *willingly* increases his own Personal Death Awareness and looks his mortality squarely in the face, he seldom prefers to return to his previous state of unawareness. The exercises in the book are set up to help you experience a higher PDA.

To understand some of the implications of having a high, low, or moderate PDA, look at three people with whom I've worked who fall into each of these categories. Two of these people died from terminal diseases, but their experiences are still relevant to so-called "healthy" people. In a sense all of us are "terminal." It's certain we're all going to die eventually—whether tomorrow in an auto accident, or next year of cancer or a heart attack, or thirty years from now, quietly, of old age.

1. **Very Low Personal Death Awareness.** Sam was a fifty-five-year-old man. In the past, he had not been able to stand hospitals, funerals, or wakes. Both he and his wife, Edna, avoided doctors whenever possible. He was admitted to the hospital with gas and back pains, and the attending physician returned a diagnosis of advanced terminal stomach cancer.

Although another member of his family and a close friend had both died of cancer, Sam refused to acknowledge the diagnosis. "The people we know who died of cancer got it after being injured," he rationalized on several occasions. "One of them was struck on the chest by the branch from a tree, and got lung cancer. The other guy was a printer who worked a lot with ink and spilled it all over himself. That gave him leukemia. But I never had any accident, so how could I have the same thing they had?"

In the next few months he lost forty-five pounds, was in intense pain, and experienced enlarged lymph nodes and a swelling belly. He continued to be puzzled by his illness, and his wife supported his denials of his poor prognosis for recovery. "You'll be up and around in no time," she told him. "Just do what these doctors tell you and get some rest, and I know you'll be all right."

He had always been an aggressive businessman who extolled efficiency and hard work as prime virtues. "I expect I'll be back to work in another month or so," he insisted.

But Sam's condition was hopeless and the medical staff did not expect him to recover. One day before he died, he told a nurse, "I'll be getting better pretty soon. All I need is a good laxative to get this swelling stomach back to normal."

Sam's denial of death created a series of unnecessary problems for himself and his family. For one thing, even when he should have been aware that something was seriously wrong with him, he postponed seeking treatment. Had he taken a realistic look at his own mortality, he might have sought professional help earlier and still be alive today.

Sam also refused to affirm his own religious beliefs. He was a Roman Catholic, yet he did not reach out for the support that his priest and the hospital chaplain were willing to give him. He failed to take advantage of the reservoirs of spiritual knowledge that might have expanded his understanding of his situation.

When he denied his own death, he failed to prepare his wife, Edna, for living alone.

There were no preparations for a funeral and burial. Sam's widow, reluctant to acknowledge that he was dead, refused to spend much time with the funeral director and finally paid much more than she might have. Sam could have settled all these matters for a reasonable cost long before he died.

Sam died without a will. As a result, his funds were tied up in lengthy court proceedings. Edna found herself having to wrestle with details that he could have easily resolved in an hour or two if he had acknowledged his mortality and acted, rather than postponed the decisions about his estate for the tomorrow that never came.

Sam left an emotionally-unprepared widow who, even for several months after his burial, spoke of him as though he were away on a business trip. His denial of his limited life span resulted in considerable waste of the last few months of his life and caused a trail of unnecessary expenses and administrative headaches. Sam's life-style—his previous stress on the importance of marital love, efficiency in his daily affairs, and a firm religious faith—was abandoned in his death style of denial.

2. **Very High Personal Death Awareness.**   Lisa, a twenty-seven-year-old schoolteacher, found herself constantly preoccupied with thoughts of her own death. Not only did these thoughts cause her a great deal of anxiety, but because of her fear, there were days when she couldn't make it out of bed to go to work.

She had a recurring dream that a huge, black, shapeless force hovered over her. The force would come down on top of her and take her breath away. She would wake up short of breath, and it was difficult for her to get back to sleep.

When she was twenty-five, Lisa had come down with a case of infectious hepatitis—a fairly common liver disease. Although this illness left her with no residual liver damage, she felt that it had. She often returned to her physician for additional liver tests. The tests came out consistently negative, but Lisa refused to believe him. She preferred to see herself as damaged and thought she was going to die in the very near future.

She wanted very much to talk with others about her fear of a shortened life, but found that her friends didn't want to discuss it. This made her feel angry and very much alone. What made it particularly difficult was that for years Lisa had played a "Dear Abby" role with her friends, always being available to listen to their problems. "Now when I need someone to listen to me," she said, "no one is around."

In order to find a sympathetic person who would listen to her and take her seriously, she began psychotherapy. In therapy, she was able to learn why she had become so preoccupied with her own death.

Lisa's father had died when she was thirteen. For a number of years her father had been an alcoholic, estranged from Lisa and her family. "I can well remember riding on the bus and seeing my father stretched out on the steps of a bar, dead drunk. I really hated him for that. At the same time, I felt sorry for him."

One day Lisa arrived home from school to find the family gathered together in the house making plans for her father's funeral. He had been found dead in a hotel room. The family was so angry with the deceased father for the way he had deserted them that they decided to get the funeral over with as soon as possible. They chose to have no service, to cremate the body, and to spread his ashes. Lisa was the only one who wanted something better for him, but since she was the youngest child in the family, no one paid her any attention. "It wasn't fair. What a crummy way to die. Without a headstone, no one would ever know that he had ever lived." She felt angry and helpless in her frustration.

During therapy, Lisa got in touch with her obsession with and fear of death. She had been afraid that she would end up like her father—with no one caring that she was dead.

Her preoccupation with chronic liver disease was her way of identifying with her father who had damaged his liver with his heavy drinking. She was able to work through her problem and bring her extremely high and debilitating Personal Death Awareness to a more manageable level.

3. Moderate Personal Death Awareness.   Jack, a thirty-year-old with a terminal kidney ailment, chose to accept his limited life span. The father of six children, he wasn't happy about dying, and he held out hope perhaps even longer than was reasonable. But he didn't fool himself by pretending he was going to live forever.

Jack had had two kidney transplants, one from his father and another from a cadaver. Neither one worked out because of his body's susceptibility to infection. After several months of intermittent hospitalization, he realized he might not pull through. But he wasn't willing to give up hope at that point, especially since his doctors continued to give him some encouragement. He began to sit in the hospital hallway and watch the elevator in the hope that an anonymous donor would appear.

Even though Jack continued to watch and wait, the hoped-for donor never appeared. He even talked about putting an advertisement in the paper for a donor, as one might do for blood donations. He constantly set goals for himself: "A donor will come in this month. Then I'll have the transplant, and by next month I'll be out of here."

Finally, he realized the donor would never arrive. His body's ability to combat infection decreased, and the inevitability of death dawned on him. Jack's first reaction was irritability: he lashed out at his nurses—uncharacteristic behavior for a person as good-natured as he was. He had become a successful salesman through his ability to get along with people, to make them like him under almost any circumstances.

Then his irritation passed, and he assumed a level-headed, realistic attitude toward his limited life span. He and his wife, Ruth, began to discuss their situation frankly. He had given her thirteen yellow roses for their first anniversary, and then a potted plant for each anniversary thereafter. But during his last stay in the hospital, he said, "This year, I want you to have a potted plant. But I think you're going to have to buy it for yourself." With that, they both began to cry. This expression of feeling helped open up communication so that they could make plans for the present and the future.

One day, a nurse walked in on them and found them discussing their marriage, what it had meant to them, and what the future would be like for their six children. During the weeks before he died, Jack brought up every conceivably relevant topic that he felt Ruth should know about. They discussed ways to arrange for mortgage payments to be made so she wouldn't lose the house after he died. Since she had always relied on him for transportation, he insisted that she get herself a driver's license and buy an inexpensive car. He also passed all of his little domestic chores and financial responsibilities to Ruth while he still had several weeks left, so that her transition to head of the household would be easier.

Then came the toughest topic of all: He told her how he wanted to be buried and insisted that he would be unhappy if she spent more than the minimum amount of money on the service, casket, and cemetery plot. "I want the money we save on the funeral to go for the kids," he told her. "Use it for their education."

Although not particularly religious, Jack had always been concerned about the welfare of others and had devoted his spare time to the Boy Scouts and other social service projects. So as his life drew to a close, it was natural for him to want to continue this altruism, to affirm the values of his life in his death. "Ruth, we never talked about this much because I guess I never expected to die," he said. "But I want you to be sure my eyes are donated to people who need them. I lived a little longer because of two kidney transplants, and I want some other people to have the same break I did."

Jack had always been close to his wife and children, perhaps because his own family life had been unsatisfactory. As his death drew nearer, he grew closer to Ruth and the six children.

Jack and Ruth talked seriously about how much they meant to each other and explained to the children exactly what was happening. He told them about the dialysis unit that had been cleansing his blood and keeping him alive between transplants. The oldest child, nine-year-old Sandy, gave a talk to her school class about kidney transplants and dialysis. Although the youngest children had trouble understanding exactly what death meant, all of them talked about it with their parents.

After Jack died, the children finally decided that they would assume responsibility for caring for their father's cemetery plot. One of the boys bought two geraniums for the grave, and the others made regular visits to clear the weeds.

Which of these three people did you most identify with? Probably most of us would say we'd *want* to be like Jack, but *know* we're more like Sam. There seem to be two main reasons why we keep our Personal Death Awareness at a low level. The first and most obvious is that we want to keep our level of anxiety about the threat of non-being, or non-existence, at a low, manageable point. Most people aren't sure what comes after death, but they suspect it's nothingness, and that's not a very pleasant thought.

But there's another reason for keeping the personal awareness level down—the idea that it's futile to think about the inevitable. As Ben Franklin said: "In this world nothing is certain but death and taxes." Or as you might put it, "There's nothing I can do about death, so why think about it? I don't have any choices."

That's where you're wrong. There are many choices open to you. You certainly don't have a choice of *whether* to die or not, but you can exercise quite a few other options.

You can choose:

- How you view death.
- To recognize you have a limited life span and begin to order your life on that basis.
- To let an understanding of your death intensify and improve your present relationships.
- What to do with your body when you're finished with it.
- How you want to be remembered by friends and family.
- Where you would like to die.
- To fear death less.
- To learn to talk more comfortably about death.
- To get the psychological upper hand over a terminal illness.
- Not to continue living on artificial, extraordinary support systems.
- Whether or not to end your own life.
- Whether or not to draw up a will.
- Whether or not to carry life insurance.
- To develop resources for confronting death.

To help you get more involved in this idea of choices, eight different types of death, based on case studies of people of various ages and backgrounds, are listed below. Look them over and decide which death would be most suitable for you, and also which you would *least* like to experience.

1. Mary died at age eighty-seven following a brief illness, at home with her family around her. Her relatives loved and cared for her, but she had felt increasingly useless during the last fifteen years of her life.

2. George died at age sixty-nine, working at a job which he enjoyed and from which he refused to retire. He had always wanted to die "in the saddle," and most people felt this is just what happened.

3. Cal died at age fifty-seven in the hospital after a rather painful illness involving several hospitalizations. He was alerted enough in advance of his death so that he could tie up all the loose ends in his estate and prepare his family for his departure.

4. Edgar died in a nursing home at age seventy-two, six months following the death of his spouse of fifty years. The doctors said he died of a broken heart.

5. Henry was walking out of a downtown bank when he got

caught in the crossfire of bullets between police and bank robbers. He was fatally shot and died immediately on the street at age forty-eight.

6. Betty died at age thirty-seven when the car in which she was riding was struck by a speeding auto driven by teen-age joyriders. She left a husband of the same age, and two small children.

7. Carrie died at age thirty of an overdose of barbiturates. She had gone through a series of unsuccessful love affairs and found that each one left her more depressed than the one before. Her friends said what she wanted most out of life was to get married, but she had eventually given up hope and foresaw only the bleak prospect of spinsterhood.

8. Keith, a single man, died at age twenty-three when a kidney which he had received through transplantation failed. He had endured many hospitalizations during his protracted illness but still managed to spread cheer among his family, friends, and the hospital staff that attended him.

Glance back over these eight experiences so that you'll have them firmly in mind. Then write down your choices.

The death I would *most* prefer for myself is number _____

The death I would *least* prefer for myself is number _____

The reasons for my choices are: _____

You probably found it easy to pick the types of death that you would *not* want for yourself. But did you have difficulty picking a death you *would* want? If so, you can be sure you have a lot of company. Because death is such a very personal matter, let me suggest that you try to design your own death—a death that would be suitable and appropriate for you, or as Avery Weisman says, "a death that you could live with." You have a style of life which you call you own. What would be your style of death?

To help you in designing a death which might be appropriate for yourself, take a few minutes to compose your own obituary-eulogy. No, don't close the book yet! Many of my students who have taken the time for this exercise have been impressed with its value, especially with the way it makes death personal for them.

You can use your own format or the one suggested below. If you use the one below, take your time and fill in the blanks thoughtfully.

OBITUARY-EULOGY

_____ died today at the age of _____
[Your full name]

A native of _____ , he/she died _____
[Your Birthplace]   [How you might die]

_____

_____

He/she is best remembered for _____
[How people will remember you]

_____

_____

_____

He/she is survived by _____
[Who in your family will live longer than you?]

_____

_____

Details of the funeral and the burial are as follows: _____

_____

_____

_____
[What kind of funeral and burial do you want?]

What was it like for you to compose your own obituary? Did you feel anxious or upset? Did any of the questions make you think about things you had refused or neglected to think about before? Look back at some of the first exercises you did in this chapter. Did you increase or decrease your estimates of your life span in your obituary?

How did you see yourself dying? Was it a so-called "natural" death, a terminal illness, or a quick, violent death, as in an accident or homicide? Perhaps you chose a self-inflicted death like suicide?

Some people find how they want to be remembered a particularly hard question, so they insert something funny. Humor can eliminate the sting, the uncomfortable feelings invoked by a serious issue.

In writing your own obituary one of the most difficult details is listing survivors. It's fairly easy for most people to conceive of living longer than their parents and not living as long as their children. But when it comes to surviving brothers and sisters, that's a much harder matter. Who among your siblings still living do you expect to die before you? Who will outlive you? If you are married, do you anticipate outliving your spouse? The statistics, as you probably know, show that most wives tend to outlive their husbands by several years.

Did you choose a large or small funeral, or any at all? Were you cremated or buried? You may say your final send-off hardly matters because you won't be aware of it. But when most people are honest with themselves, they admit they want a say about their funerals, if only to keep the costs down and preserve their estates.

Now that you've increased your Personal Death Awareness through some hard thinking and by doing several exercises, what feelings are you experiencing? Take a moment to explore your reactions and make a note of them.

Right now I am feeling mostly:

_____ anxious	_____ frightened
_____ calm	_____ oppressed
_____ tense	_____ confused
_____ sick	_____ bored
_____ angry	_____ interested
_____ happy	_____ other
_____ amused	

Think of three people you know well with whom you might share these feelings. Write down their names and anticipate how they might respond to your feelings by checking the appropriate boxes.

Response:	Very helpful	Somewhat helpful	Not helpful
My first choice: _____ Name	_____	_____	_____
My second choice: _____ Name	_____	_____	_____
My third choice: _____ Name	_____	_____	_____

If you checked the "not helpful" box for any of these people, *why* do you think they would react negatively? Could it be because they keep their own PDA quite low?

In the foregoing exercises and case illustrations we've seen that increasing your own Personal Death Awareness—breaking free from fear and denial—can have several concrete benefits. The most obvious is that you'll be able to make choices about your own death. You only have one chance to die. Don't muff it!

But an awareness of your own mortality can also help you live a more effective life in the here and now:

- You can deal with feelings and not have to hide them.
- You can identify what it is specifically about dying which is causing you anxiety. Once you've pinpointed the cause, you can proceed to do something about it.
- You can take more advantage of opportunities which happen your way. A healthy Personal Death Awareness will prevent you from postponing until tomorrow tasks which can *only* be done today. Tomorrow may be too late.
- If you remember that you and your loved ones won't live forever, you can have more significant, less superficial, personal relationships. But if you postpone expressing appreciation and love, death may intervene to make your temporary delay a permanent thing. Or if you harbor longstanding grudges, the grave may prevent them from being resolved. In psychotherapy sessions, I often have to work with people who have profound resentments which they never expressed to their parents. The parents are now dead, but the resentments linger on and have to be worked out in therapy.

I think psychologist Rollo May understood the place of death in life when he wrote, "The confronting of death gives the most positive reality to life itself. It makes the individual existence real, absolute, and concrete. Death is the one fact of my life which is not relative but absolute, and my awareness of this gives my existence and what I do each hour an absolute quality."[3]

People often ask me if working with the dying isn't a depressing experience. It can be a *sad* experience, especially with a person to whom I am particularly close. But on the positive side, working with the dying has increased my awareness of the brevity of life and the importance of living my life now and not postponing things until tomorrow. As you allow yourself to experience a healthy increase in your own Personal Death Awareness, you too may find yourself reaching out for life with a new healthy zest.

1. Avery D. Weisman, *On Dying and Denying* (New York: Behavioral Publications, 1973), 63,65.
2. E. and M. Polster, *Gestalt Therapy Integrated* (New York: Brunner/Mazel, 1973).
3. Rollo May, *Existence* (New York: Basic Books, 1958), 49.

Chapter Two

SKETCHING THE UNKNOWN

"The grim reaper," "Jordan's bank," "the journey's end," "that dreamless sleep," "the way of all flesh," "going home," and "dust" are a few images which have been used to describe the end of life, that last unknown which has a different outline in each of our imaginations. The picture that you harbor in your mind may be frightening or comforting, but perhaps you've never even thought about death in graphic terms. It's likely that many of your conscious fears and anxieties are rooted in a shadowy image of death—an ominous anticipation of the unknown that lurks on the edge of your subconscious.

To get a clearer idea of *your* concept of death, become an artist for a few moments. Take a pencil, pen, or better yet, some colored crayons if you have them handy, and in the space below draw death as you imagine it. Don't spend a lot of time thinking about it. Begin drawing here and on the next page and see what emerges.

MY PICTURE OF DEATH

There are a variety of possibilities for this sketch of death. Each image reflects something important about the artist's attitude toward his own mortality.

Some people just stare at the paper and draw nothing. They are probably suffering from a strong tendency to deny death, perhaps in order to keep their PDA low. If you're still in this category even after reading the last chapter, take a risk. Draw *something!* There are choices open to you if you bring your own Personal Death Awareness to a higher level.

Other people draw a simple circle, to suggest that death may be a channel to something else, but they're not sure just what. A few are so certain that there's nothing after this life that they draw a box or circle and black it in, to indicate that their image of death is a final barrier. A billowing, cloud-shaped mass is another abstract image that may indicate a half-comforting, half-threatening envelopment that overtakes the individual at the end of life.

Some have chosen specific objects, such as a door or passageway— a sure sign that the artist imagines death as an introduction to some other form of life. Others sketch an animal figure, like a hovering bat, to suggest a threatening image of death. Still other drawings involve figures of people—happy, sad, ominous, indifferent, or comforting. One young woman drew her own tombstone and then sketched a replica of her own smiling face in the sun, trees, flowers, and fish in a pond that surrounded her grave. She saw herself merging into the universe in some happy way. A young intern at the Johns Hopkins Medical School drew a strictly medical image—an electrocardiogram line which showed a normal heartbeat, then a spasm of the heart, and finally a flat line indicating death.

Study your drawing for a few moments and consider what you think it indicates about your attitude toward what your own death will be like. In what ways do you think your image of death affects your present life?

To get a clearer sense of your concept of death, complete the following sentence by writing the first response that comes to mind:

When I think of death, I think of _____

Did your answer involve a concrete image, an abstract concept, or some feeling? Some people think of an image like the kind you sketched. Others immediately recall a friend or relative who has died. Still others experience a feeling—butterflies in the stomach, relief, resignation, horror.

Elisabeth Kubler-Ross and I examined the attitudes of five thousand health professionals of all ages who were asked to write the first thing that came to their minds when they thought of death.

Younger people, on the whole, saw death in more negative terms, perhaps because they felt they had their whole lives ahead of them. They tended to describe death as the end of existence, a separation or loss, an empty void, or a general feeling of unhappiness. Older people, on the other hand, had a more hopeful attitude toward the end of life. Death for them was frequently seen as heaven, relief, escape, new life, and reunion.

Our study also indicated factors other than age which were important in influencing a person's concept of death. The Protestant health professionals were more likely to think of death in terms of heaven, while Jews saw it as a cycle or a void which involved loss and separation.

The professional training of the interviewees also seemed to influence their thinking. Many of the nurses associated death with a dysphoric feeling—a sense of being unwell or unhappy. The physicians frequently thought of the end of life as the end of everything; or they responded with the name of a specific person they knew who had died.

The most positive association to death came from medical paraprofessionals who saw death as a release, and ministers who associated it with heaven or renewal. The mental health workers—perhaps because their work is concerned mainly with introspection and self-knowledge—tended to connect the general notion of death with thoughts of their own deaths. Social workers frequently regarded death as a loss, a void, separation, or the end of everything.

Only two percent of those we surveyed denied *ever* thinking of death. The majority indicated in some fashion that the main issue that death posed for them was whether there was *new* life or *no* life beyond the grave.

One approach to understanding death is to *personify* it. From your personal relationships, you know that the better you get to know a person—his physical features, emotional quirks and reactions to a variety of situations—the better you're able to understand him. Take some time to consider death as a personal acquaintance (if not a friend) by coming up with a personality profile. Think about each of these questions for a few moments, and then check the responses which seem most right to you.

If death were a person I would see death as:

_____	young	_____	male
_____	middle-aged	_____	female
_____	old	_____	sexless

Death would be dressed in _____
with a face that looks like _____

Death would have the following mental and physical characteristics. Circle the number on each line which indicates the degree to which death partakes of each set of qualities (e.g., if you conceive of death as half warm and half cold, circle "3", and so on).

		1	2	3	4	5	
1.	warm	1	2	3	4	5	cold
2.	soft	1	2	3	4	5	hard
3.	kind	1	2	3	4	5	cruel
4.	practical	1	2	3	4	5	scatterbrained
5.	safe	1	2	3	4	5	dangerous
6.	stable	1	2	3	4	5	unstable
7.	pleasant	1	2	3	4	5	obnoxious
8.	loving	1	2	3	4	5	hateful
9.	decisive	1	2	3	4	5	wishy-washy
10.	just	1	2	3	4	5	unjust
11.	rational	1	2	3	4	5	irrational
12.	tender	1	2	3	4	5	tough
13.	intelligent	1	2	3	4	5	stupid
14.	imaginative	1	2	3	4	5	unimaginative
15.	witty	1	2	3	4	5	humorless
16.	exciting	1	2	3	4	5	dull
17.	humble	1	2	3	4	5	arrogant
18.	cautious	1	2	3	4	5	careless

19.	honest	1	2	3	4	5	deceitful
20.	relaxed	1	2	3	4	5	tense
21.	quiet	1	2	3	4	5	noisy
22.	unselfish	1	2	3	4	5	selfish
23.	sexy	1	2	3	4	5	unsexy
24.	sociable	1	2	3	4	5	aloof
25.	generous	1	2	3	4	5	stingy
26.	cheerful	1	2	3	4	5	sulky
27.	fast-moving	1	2	3	4	5	slow-moving
28.	smooth-skinned	1	2	3	4	5	rough-skinned
29.	beautiful	1	2	3	4	5	ugly
30.	healthy	1	2	3	4	5	sick
31.	rounded	1	2	3	4	5	angular
32.	weak	1	2	3	4	5	strong
33.	passive	1	2	3	4	5	active
34.	small	1	2	3	4	5	large
35.	good	1	2	3	4	5	bad
36.	wet	1	2	3	4	5	dry

Now take your pencil and connect each of your responses in the above exercise with a continuous line down the page. Does your line rest more on the right- or left-hand side of the page? If most of your answers fall on the left-hand side, you conceive of death as a rather pleasant, non-threatening, even friendly sort of person. But if your personality line travels mostly along the right-hand side, death in your opinion, tends to be tough, cruel, aggressive, arbitrary, and overbearing—not the sort of individual you'd want to meet for a pleasant evening of conversation. If your line moved back and forth across the page or stayed close to the middle so that neither side of the personality profile predominates, then death has ambivalent properties for you.

Perhaps you're wondering how your idea of death as a person compares with that of other people. Robert Kastenbaum, one of the more creative researchers in the field of death and dying, asked a number of his college students this question: "If death were a person, what do you think it would look like?"[1]

Some of his students saw death as a macabre figure. One wrote, "Death is a walking death. He is a male, about eighty-nine years old, and is very bent over. His hair is scraggly, his face is wrinkled, almost not recognizable as human flesh. His eyes are sunken, his teeth are rotting. . . ."

Other students envisioned death as a gentle comforter, who sometimes looked like an elderly man or grandfather-type, such as the popular conceptions of "Father Time." A slightly different idea of a comforter popped into the mind of a young female student, who said, "Physically, death would be male. He would be very strong, very powerful. He would be quiet; he would speak very softly and gently. He would be light-haired and have darker skin; that is, not a fair, whitish complexion. . . ."

Death was also imagined as an automaton, an objective, unfeeling instrument in human guise. One such description of death went like this: "Lean, pale, clothed in the color of nothing; sexless; not senile but older-looking, about sixty years of age. He is unthinking and automatic, inured to and bored by suffering, having no moral values or need of them." Although seen as human, this vision of death has no feelings and goes about its business in a matter-of-fact way.

Another negative personification of death was the enticing deceiver who, like the serpent in the Garden of Eden, promises good things but actually leads the way to ultimate destruction. Although each of the 421 people that Dr. Kastenbaum questioned endowed death with certain peculiar, individualized features, the most common idea was that death was a late middle-aged or elderly man who was "gentle and well meaning."

Do you find that your ideas of death as a person are similar to these, or is your mental image quite different? Even if there are some similarities, your own personification of death, which should by now be fairly clear in your mind, is probably unique. This concept is fluid and will more than likely change a number of times during your life. I believe that there are at least three major factors that influence your present notions of death—your *age*, your *personal death history*, and the *social subculture* to which you belong. Let's take a detailed look at each of these influences.

Some of the most obvious examples of how age can influence a person's concept of death occur among children. A classic study in this field is one done by Maria Nagy, who studied 378 Hungarian children, an equal number of boys and girls ranging in age from three to ten years.[2] After asking them to draw death and then talk about what their drawings meant, she identified three major stages in the approach these children took to their own mortality.

The first stage lasted until age five. The preschool children usually didn't recognize death as final or permanent. Instead, it was a departure, a deep sleep, or some other temporarily absent condition. They believed death was the same thing as life, but life under somewhat different circumstances.

The young boys and girls between the ages of five and nine began to personify death in some way, either as a separate person or as a dead person. Death became something quite different from life for this age group, and they seemed to comprehend that death is final or permanent. But it still is not inevitable for the child himself at this stage. There is a sense that if you keep on your toes, you can sidestep the Grim Reaper in some way. Death, in other words, is not a necessary experience for everybody.

At about age nine or ten, the child moves into the final phase of his thinking and realizes that death is final, permanent, and inevitable for everyone, including himself. But even if a child learns at this early age that death is inevitable, his way of thinking about the experience will continue to be influenced by his age as he grows older.

Adolescents and young adults usually are so enmeshed in their identity crises as they try to understand who they are and how they fit into the world that they "cannot see the future for the teens," as Dr. Edwin S. Shneidman puts it.[3] Shneidman noticed that young people have trouble writing their own obituaries. They have "understandable difficulty in objectifying themselves," he explained. "Youth is not life's time for death. [A] sample of elicited obituaries from college students is further proof . . . that the young—perhaps only the young—are immortal."

The changing attitudes of a friend of mine illustrate this approach of the young adult to death. He kept a journal of his thoughts and spiritual experiences over a period of years and made a number of entries on death. When he was in college, the entries generally involved a denial or lack of concern with death and life after death. He realized that a rejection of the idea of a life after death conflicted with his traditional Christian convictions and his belief that he could communicate with a personal God who was concerned about his welfare. "Although I know that I have to die someday," he wrote, "I'm not interested in thinking about it. As for immortality, or life after death, I can't imagine it. I guess I don't really believe in it. . . . At any rate, my death doesn't make any difference in my present relationship with God."

During his twenties, after he got married and lived through rocket attacks in Vietnam, his notion of death changed. "I guess there's about a thirty percent chance that there's a life after death," he wrote in his diary. "But I still think that it's more likely than not that death is the end. There's probably nothing afterwards. I know this attitude is inconsistent with my faith in a personal God, but that's the way I feel."

Just a few years later, though, when this fellow reached his early thirties, his attitude changed radically. His belief in an afterlife flip-flopped so that he was "seventy percent sure, thirty percent unsure" about a continued form of existence after death. Soon after, he became "virtually certain" that there was a life after death. He attributes this change in his concept of death to a deepening personal spiritual commitment. But another prime reason was probably the fact that he had moved beyond adolescence into a different age group.

Some studies have revealed a tendency among the elderly in our society to view death as having the characteristics of a friend, a comforter who comes to take the person to a better existence than he is now experiencing. The study that Elisabeth Kubler-Ross and I conducted with health professionals also suggested a more benign attitude toward death among the older people. But John W. Riley cautions against accepting this idea as an absolute generalization. He surveyed 1,482 adults and found that "older people are a little more likely than younger to agree that 'death is like a long sleep' or 'death is sometimes a blessing.' But there is little indication that such attitudes constitute a general set of views which change with age and which condone a passive acceptance of death."[4] So if we want to understand exactly why we conceive of death in the way we do, it's necessary to look beyond age.

A second key influence on how you see death—a factor associated consciously or subconsciously with the kind of picture you did at the beginning of this chapter—is what I call your "personal death history." Your death history involves the deaths which you have seen and experienced thus far in your life, including not only people you have known but animals as well. Take your own death history by filling in the blanks below.

PERSONAL DEATH HISTORY

1. The first death that I experienced was the death of _____ _____

2. I was _____ years old.
3. At that time I felt _____
4. I was most curious about _____
5. The things that frightened me most were _____
6. The feelings I have now as I think of that death are _____ _____

7. The first funeral I ever attended was for _____ _____

8. The most intriguing thing about the funeral was _____ _____

9. I was most scared at the funeral by _____ _____

10. The first personal acquaintance of my own age who died was _____

11. I remember thinking _____
12. I lost my first parent when I was _____ years old.
13. The death of this parent was especially significant because _____

14. The most recent death I experienced was when _____ died _____ years ago.
15. The most traumatic death I ever experienced was _____ _____

16. At age ____ I personally came closest to death when _____ _____

You may have left some of the questions above blank because these days, with greater longevity in our society, it's not uncommon for a person to reach adulthood without experiencing the death of a close friend or family member. In teaching a university course on death, I find that many of the students in the class, even though they were in their late teens or early twenties, have never experienced the death of anyone close to them.

But when that first death of a loved one strikes, your attitude toward death (and toward the meaning of life as well) will almost certainly change. About a year ago, a friend of mine lost his father through a heart attack. Two months after the funeral, he told an acquaintance, "Well, it was tough to have to go through that, but I think I'm over it now."

His acquaintance, who had also lost his father, replied, "You never get over it. I know."

What this second man was saying was that even after the period of initial sorrow and grief has passed, the death of a loved one inevitably changes the course of your life. It's not possible to rely on the deceased for advice, support, praise, or compassion.

The death of a loved one is almost always followed by a sense of loss of continuity with the past, and the survivor must either become more self-sufficient, or find another individual on whom he can lean to fulfill certain emotional needs. As the meaning of your friend's or relative's death becomes clearer with the passage of time, you find you are better able to understand your own death—the fact that you will be separated from *your* loved ones and that they will experience the same sense of separation and loss that you yourself have experienced.

My own son, Michael, experienced his first family death recently at the age of nine. After her father had suddenly taken seriously ill, my wife had been called to the West Coast. Several days later she telephoned me to say that her father had died, and to request that I tell Michael. I wanted to be sure that I took the time to help him have a positive experience.

That evening I sat down with Michael in the living room and told him that his Papa Earl had died. I also told him that there would be a memorial service the following day. "What's a memorial service, Dad?" he asked.

I explained to him that a memorial service was held so people who knew and loved the deceased could come together and remember the good things about the person who was gone. "What things do you remember best about Papa Earl?"

As we began to talk, most of his memories centered about his grandfather as he had been in recent years when he had been physically impaired by a series of minor strokes. Soon however, his memories stretched further back to a time when he was very small and we had spent a summer with his grandparents in San Francisco while I was studying at Stanford University.

As we talked and remembered, we both felt sad. I tried to help Michael see that sadness and tears were most appropriate to our memories and to this occasion. It was a meaningful experience which he and I shared together that evening, and I always remember it with great warmth.

The following week we drove to the airport to pick up my wife. We had just parked the car in the garage when Michael piped up with, "How was the funeral Mom? Was it good?"

Coolly she replied, "If you can call a funeral good!"

Later, when I told her about our little memorial service in the living room that evening, she understood the reason for his positive, even enthusiastic attitude toward the funeral. He was learning to accept death as a necessary part of life, and memorial services as sorrowful, but also meaningful and affirmative experiences. He had passed the first milestone in his own personal death history.

A third important influence in molding your mental picture of death is the social subculture to which you belong, which includes religious, educational, and family influences. Traditional Christians in our society believe in a resurrection of the body after death for the faithful and an afterlife in communion with God. Among Jews there has been no unanimity on the existence of life after death. Many agnostics and atheists mirror the prevailing attitudes of their social circle by declaring, "When you're dead, you're dead." Contemporary atheistic humanists, who completely reject the idea of an afterlife, may still conduct memorial services for their dead. But those attending these services regard the body only as a lifeless object which should be venerated briefly for what it once was, but not for what it will become.

The social influences which shape our concepts of death are also echoed in other cultures throughout the world. As John W. Riley says, there is "no known society [where] the individual is left to face death completely uninitiated. He is provided with beliefs about 'the dead', and he is offered a range of theories about his own probable fate after death."[5]

A good example of the importance of such cultural influences outside our own American society involves an incident which occurred on the island of Rotuma, which lies about 300 miles north of the Fiji group on the Western fringe of Polynesia.[6] A Rotuma native, while lolling around one evening, asked some visitors: "What do you think is better, to be alive or to be dead?"

After his guests had given their answers, the young man stated his opinion. A dead person, he said, no longer has to worry about the future or about work. He can just rest, for death is similar to dreamless sleep.

This answer was consistent with the general attitude the Rotumans have that death, like their life, is rather passive. Death is a form of sleep, a sensual experience similar to the idyllic life lived under a warm sun where food is plentiful and easily obtained. In other words, the young man's concept of death was shaped in large part by the values of his society. If he were asked to draw a picture of death, as you were at the beginning of this chapter, he would probably sketch a figure snoozing comfortably under a warm sun on a beach.

Turn back again to the drawing you did of death. How do you think your age, personal death history, and cultural milieu influenced that sketch? Do you think you would draw death differently if you had to do it again? What has encouraged you to change your mind?

If your concept has changed, it's likely that your mental picture of death is more positive now than it was at first. The more we examine a potentially ominous subject, the less threatening it often seems. A series of unhappy experiences in your death history, or perhaps some influences relating to your age or social group may have been encouraging you to keep your Personal Death Awareness excessively low. Now you may find it easier to look your own death in the face. This is the first step in freeing yourself both to make more death-related choices during your life, and also to avoid destructive emotional disturbances that can arise from a low Personal Death Awareness.

1. Robert Kastenbaum and R. Aisenberg, *The Psychology of Death* (New York: Springer Publishing Co., Inc., 1972).
2. Maria Nagy, "The Child's View of Death," *Journal of Genetic Psychology,* 73(1948), 3-27.
3. Edwin S. Shneidman, "Can a Young Person Write His Own Obituary?" *Life-Threatening Behavior,* 2(1972), 262-267.

4. John W. Riley Jr., "What People Think About Death," in *The Dying Patien*
   O. G. Brim, Jr., H. E. Freeman, S. Levine, and N. A. Scotch (New York: Ru
   Foundation, 1970).
5. John W. Riley Jr., "Death and Bereavement," in *International Encyclopedia of the
   Social Sciences* (New York: Free Press, 1968).
6. A. Howard and R. A. Scott, "Cultural Values and Attitudes Toward Death," *Journ
   of Existentialism*, 6(Winter, 1965), 161-174.

Chapter Three

PDA AND YOUR MENTAL HEALTH

Your death is as much a part of your life as the book you're now holding, or as the person sitting in the room with you. Some day—perhaps thirty years from now, perhaps next month, perhaps tomorrow—your body will permanently cease to function. You'll experience the ultimate earthly separation from your family, friends, and favorite activities.

Because death is such a serious, disturbing business, you may find you can't think about it too long without getting anxious or depressed. You say, "I'm not going to think about my death. I'm going to proceed as though I'll live forever." This denial of your own death is natural and necessary—up to a point. If your Personal Death Awareness becomes a preoccupation, you can become immobilized—completely ineffectual in your daily work and personal relationships. Without some denial, a sense of helplessness, powerlessness, and vulnerability will overwhelm you.

We all experience some feelings of vulnerability from earliest childhood. The small child realizes that he can't make it alone, that he has to depend on others for his very survival. As adults, we learn to be self-sufficient but we also recognize that death is the ultimate assault on our power and autonomy as human beings. To be human is to exercise choices freely, and death often seems to be a forced choice, the greatest affront to our ability to control our lives.

Even though we can temper this sense of helplessness and vulnerability by denying that we're going to die, denial often fails us.

First of all, denial is ineffective because events outside your control can force your own death back into clear focus in your mind. You may read in the newspapers about someone dying in a house fire or about some senseless, random murder and suddenly realize that the same thing might happen to you. Or more likely, the death of someone close to you may make it impossible for you to ignore your own inevitable demise.

For example, when one of his parents dies, it's common for the oldest child in a family to have the sense that he's "next in line." This feeling can be especially strong if the surviving child has to take over family responsibilities that were once the province of the mother or father.

When a sibling or close contemporary dies, an individual's Personal Death Awareness becomes even more acute. A friend told me that when his brother, a hard-working man, died, he decided to retire early "because I want to be sure I enjoy life a little before I go." My friend's higher PDA prompted him to take action that would have been impossible if his natural tendency to deny his own death had prevailed.

A second problem is that denial may fail to lower subliminal PDA lurking at the edge of consciousness. I believe that many of the deep-rooted psychological disturbances that we face are related in some way to Personal Death Awareness. Even a low level PDA can encourage a sense of helplessness and vulnerability, which in turn can give rise to feelings of fear, futility, and frustration. As we attempt to cope with these feelings, the final result may be a host of behavior difficulties such as neurotic behavior, existential depression, or excessive aggression. The following diagram illustrates this pattern:

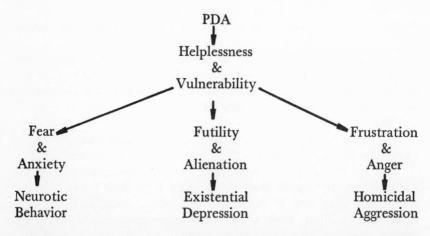

A number of prominent philosophers and psychotherapists have been struck by the connection between an awareness of one's own mortality and various emotional problems. Laura Perls, a leading

Gestalt therapist, has said, ". . . the basic problem not only of therapy but of life is how to make life livable for a being whose dominant characteristic is his awareness of himself as a unique individual on the one hand and of his mortality on the other. The first gives him a feeling of overwhelming importance and the other a feeling of *fear and frustration*. Suspended between these poles, he vibrates in a state of inevitable *tension and anxiety* that, at least to modern Western man, seems unrelievable. This causes various neurotic solutions that are prevalent not only in our patients but to a greater or lesser degree in our total culture. . . . In our Western world, *the neurotic is the man who cannot face his own dying* and therefore cannot live fully as a human being." (Emphasis added.)[1]

The late Ernest Becker, Pulitzer Prize-winning author of the *Denial of Death*, said he believed the fear of death is "the basic fear that influences all others, a fear from which no one is immune, no matter how disguised it may be."[2] He also has cited with approval therapists who stress that the ultimate foundation for all our "basic animal anxieties" is the terror we have of death.[3]

Anxiety which lies behind much neurotic behavior stems basically from a fear of separation. Children become uneasy when they're separated from their parents. The parent is the ultimate source of the child's safety and nourishment. Without the parent he feels helpless and can't survive. An acute awareness of your death in your later life may resurrect feelings of vulnerability and fear similar to those you felt as a small child, when you were threatened by the loss or absence of a parent. Neurotic behavior is an attempt to cope with these feelings of anxiety.

You may object, "But death *is real*, isn't it? So isn't it logical to feel fear or anxiety about death?

True, if someone is holding a knife at your throat, it's natural to become afraid or anxious. But even if there is no such immediate death threat, a deep-rooted sense of vulnerability may lead to serious neurotic fears and anxieties. The way some people manage these anxieties is through subconscious psychological processes that result in abnormal and sometimes bizarre behavior patterns.

Let's look at some of these neurotic behaviors in which the fear of death can be seen in the symbolic meaning of the behavior and where deaths are frequently associated with the onset of these behaviors.[4]

Phobias.   A phobia is a persistent, morbid, unreasonable fear which is exaggerated out of proportion to the danger of the dreaded object or situation. Symbolically, a phobia expresses the thought that: "If I can avoid this object or that situation, then I won't be helpless or anxious, and die." A phobia—or the focus of your anxiety on one clearly defined object—helps you reduce your general feelings of anxiety and helplessness as long as you can keep away from the dreaded object.

For example, Gerry, a young woman in her twenties, had an intense fear of bees. Her fear had begun at age twelve or thirteen, when her father told her about a boy who had died of a bee sting. But her father's story wasn't the basic cause of the phobia. The real root of her problem lay in her intense hatred of her mother, who was an alcoholic. Underlying the behavior was the thought, "I hate my mother so much I could kill her . . . but if she knew what I'm thinking, she might kill *me*." Unable to deal with the anxieties that resulted from these aggressive, hostile impulses toward her mother, she developed a phobia toward bees. In her mind, she was convinced, "Unless I avoid the bees and their sting, I might die." By avoiding the bees—a relatively easy task—she was able to avoid the anxiety surrounding her hatred and fear of her mother, and ultimately her fantasy about the deadly power her mother exercised over her.

Through psychotherapy sessions, Gerry began to understand that her hostility toward her mother would not actually create any real danger to her own existence. She also found appropriate ways of expressing her anger.

A similar kind of PDA-related phobia gripped Joan, who had a fear of falling down stairs. Behind her fear was a sense that she couldn't stand on her own two feet—a feeling that had begun at a young age when her father's death had caused her to worry that she might not be able to survive. To manage this fear of her own death, she focused her terror on stairs. Joan's husband helped her control her fear of stairs because he acted as her moral, and sometimes her physical support. But then her husband started going with another woman, and Joan's primitive fear of death surfaced again in its full intensity as a stair phobia. When confronted by a staircase, she experienced the classic signs of severe anxiety— nervousness, rapid heartbeat, tremors, cold perspiration, and a sense of weakness. The uppermost thought in her mind was to get as far away as possible from the threatening object. Her problems with her husband had intensified her phobia because she was afraid that once again a person on whom she relied heavily would be separated from her and she wouldn't be able to make it on her own.

Psychological treatment freed her to release the bottled-up anger and fear she felt toward her husband and her father. The anxiety that came from these fears of separation, and ultimately of death, soon began to dissipate.

Phobias may become attached to almost any situation or object. An abnormal fear of flying in airplanes is one of the most common. You yourself may know someone who suffers from this problem. The phobia suggests, "I'm helpless in this plane because I have no control over it; and if I'm helpless, I'll die. Therefore, I refuse to fly."

After reaching adulthood, Larry, age twenty-eight, developed an intense fear of flying. The phobia began shortly after the loss of his father. The same year his father died, he suffered a number of other separations and unpleasant changes in his life. He had broken up with his girl friend, dropped out of graduate school, and "totaled" his car in an auto accident. A number of the major supports in his life had been knocked out from under him. It was at that time that he began to be uncomfortable when flying. He said to me, "In a plane, I feel vulnerable and helpless. When I'm flying, my fate is not in my own hands." Subconsciously he was saying, "I don't have any control over whether or not I survive."

There was a certain amount of truth in his comments, but statistically speaking, it was no more realistic for him to fear travel in airplanes than in cars or on subways. During therapy, Larry confronted his fear of death directly. He soon learned to handle his feelings of vulnerability and concern about his own mortality with greater understanding and acceptance. Through hypnosis and systematic desensitization treatment, he began to travel more comfortably by air.

Compulsions.   Anxiety resulting from the fear and helplessness that accompany an excessively high PDA may also result in compulsive or obsessive behavior. Compulsions may be relatively harmless and trivial. As children, my friends and I would playfully avoid stepping on cracks while walking to school. "Step on a crack, break your mother's back!" we'd shout.

Neurotic compulsions are more serious. Some people may find that they experience undue anxiety unless they go through certain major rituals such as handwashing. A sense of comfort and relief from this anxiety depends on complying *exactly* with the compulsive behavior patterns. Symbolically, this inner need to follow compulsive procedures suggests, "If I don't do this, something bad will happen, and I may die."

Leon, a thirty-one-year-old accountant, had an insomnia problem. He said he couldn't go to sleep without first going through a certain set of bedtime rituals. His compulsion involved this step-by-step procedure:

1. Shower.
2. Brush teeth, *after* shower.
3. Dial weather information on telephone.
4. Lay out clothes for morning.
5. Lock back door first, then front door.
6. Turn off living room lights in a specific order.
7. Turn down bed covers.
8. Open bedroom window.
9. Turn off bedroom lights in a specific order.

Leon said if he skipped any of these steps or performed them out of sequence, he felt "unsafe." Apparently he believed that if he failed to give in to his compulsion, he might not wake up from his sleep. Deep in his subconscious, he was actually afraid that, without the protection of his ritualistic behavior, he might die.

As he shared his concerns, it soon became evident that the source of his compulsion was a repressed anxiety he had felt about his parents' threats to leave him as a child.

"If you're not good, we'll leave you on the side of the highway," his father had warned several times. Leon had believed him. Because he saw the outside world as a dangerous place, he believed that he might be lost forever if his parents abandoned him.

Discussions helped Leon confront his irrational fears and also enabled him to redefine the external world as a much safer place than he had imagined as a child. As he began to see that he could exercise control over his environment, he felt less helpless and vulnerable. As for his compulsion, he started omitting one ritual at a time. Even though he had a few sleepless nights, he finally found that he could go to sleep safely without performing the compulsive bedtime procedures.

Hypochondria.   A hypochondriac is preoccupied with his body and the fear of presumed diseases of various organs. His fears, which aren't based on reality, persist despite reassurances from medical experts.

Beth, a forty-eight-year-old woman whose youngest child had just gone away to college, began to suffer feelings of inadequacy and aimlessness. Because her children weren't around to occupy her time, life no longer had any meaning. Her purposelessness caused her to feel anxious and depressed, and she focused on her own personal health.

Beth always imagined that she had an ache here and a pain there. When one of her friends became ill and discussed her symptoms with her, Beth would develop the same symptoms the next day. But if she went to a doctor and was told she was all right, she refused to accept the diagnosis and headed for another doctor. Because of her imagined illnesses, she became well-known in the clinics and hospitals in her neighborhood.

Beth needed something specific to worry about, or she would have to face the ultimate issue she felt she couldn't handle—the question of what her life was all about. Her hypochondria covered up a tendency toward severe depression that would immobilize her when it surfaced. In effect, she was saying symbolically, "I've got to keep checking my body because if it's not in perfect working order, I might die." She also felt inadequate to face the deeper question: "Now that my children are gone, is my life finished? Is my death all I have to look forward to?"

During therapy she was encouraged to confront her hypochondria for what it really was—a distracting device which was preventing her from grappling with her changed status of no longer being needed as a mother. Beth finally began to concentrate more on outside activities, such as helping others through volunteer groups and church work. She found she no longer had the time or inclination to dwell on her imagined diseases, nor on the terrifying death that lay behind them.

Anxiety Reaction. This emotional problem involves a state of panic where the cause of the panic is often unknown. You may suddenly feel very uneasy and have a sense of impending disaster. Your body mobilizes its forces to meet the stress, and the result may be heart palpitations, rapid pulse, and occasional breathing difficulties. The symptoms can be limited to a few minutes or go on for days. There is a feeling that the world is a threatening place and you're unable to meet the everyday demands placed upon you.

After smoking marijuana and listening to music in a friend's apartment, a young student named Ed suddenly began feeling this kind of anxiety. He perspired profusely and felt light-headed. He feared that if he didn't flee that apartment and the people around him, he might actually faint.

Ed came in to see us at the university health services that evening. Even though he couldn't pinpoint the object of his anxiety, he described his feelings as best he could: "I thought I was in some kind of danger, and if I didn't get out of that place, something bad would happen to me."

In helping Ed come to grips with his problem, we helped him to "reality test" the situation. I asked, "So what if you do pass out? What would actually happen to you?"

"No one would help me."

"Then what?" I asked.

"I would die."

But after he thought for a few moments about his answer, he admitted that his friend would undoubtedly come to his aid. He was not as much in danger of extinction as he had thought.

During the time that we counseled him, we discovered that much of his anxiety was rooted in a repressed hostility that he felt toward his father. His father had always refused to allow him to express any anger or opposition to parental authority. When Ed was quite young, the older man used physical sanctions like spankings and after Ed got older he threatened financial reprisals, such as cutting off his college money.

Ed was operating on the subconscious notion that, "If I show anger toward my parents, they will retaliate against me in such a terrible way that my own safety, my future, my very life may be in danger."

He finally recognized that he was not in as much danger as he had thought, and he began to express his anger toward his father instead of bottling up his feelings. After an initial period of alienation, the son and father developed a healthier relationship than they had known before.

A sense of helplessness resulting from an awareness of personal mortality could lead you in a second direction, toward a sense of *futility and depression.* There is good research evidence that helplessness can lead to clinical depression. Helplessness associated with thoughts of one's death can also lead one into an existential kind of depression rooted in the notion that, because of death, life is meaningless. A good illustration of existential depression is "Beth" whose problems were described earlier.

In experiments with dogs and other animals, Dr. Martin E. P. Seligman has determined that a depression can be induced by teaching the animal to give up, or accept passively an uncomfortable, vulnerable, or even painful situation.[5] In one set of his experiments, an unharnessed dog was placed in a box and subjected to electrical shock. The animal easily found a means of escape by jumping over a side of the box. Then another dog was harnessed and subjected to the same kind of shock over a period of time. When the harness was removed, the second animal failed to jump over the barrier, but simply accepted the pain passively.[6]

This "learned helplessness," Seligman says, is similar to certain kinds of human depression. Human beings, he has found, also get depressed when they are gripped by a sense of helplessness or vulnerability.

Ernest Becker noted a connection between death awareness and depression when he wrote, "... the less you do ... the more helpless and dependent you become. The more you shrink back from the difficulties and darings of life, the more you naturally come to feel inept. ... This state is the bogging-down of depression. Fear of life leads to excessive fear of death. ... Finally, one doesn't dare to move—the patient lies in bed for days on end, not eating, letting the housework pile up, ... in some way one must pay with life and consent daily to die, to give oneself up to the risks and dangers of the world, allow oneself to be engulfed and used up. Otherwise one ends up *as though dead* in trying to avoid life and death."[7]

An excessive Personal Death Awareness may contribute to the sense of futility, helplessness, and passivity that make the depressed person feel "There's nothing I can do about anything. Life has no purpose. If I'm going to die anyway, what's the point to living?"

A sense of vulnerability and helplessness about your death could lead you in still another direction. You may get an over-bearing feeling of *frustration* and find the only way to deal with the resulting anger is to take some excessively aggressive action against another person. If the sense of frustration is intense enough, violence may result. Being vulnerable and yet impotent to act can cause a rage similar to the rage displayed by infants who are unable to affect their environment. In lashing out against others, you say symbolically, "You're dead—not me. If I can wield death and make it work for me, then maybe death will leave me alone. The more people like you that I can hurt, the more I'll decrease my chances of being destroyed. I will destroy you before you destroy me."

All of these aberrant behaviors associated with fear, futility, and frustration are attempts to deal with the sense of vulnerability and helplessness that can accompany the dread of personal death. None of the solutions is adequate, however, because even though such behavior may lower vulnerability temporarily, the cost is too high in terms of personal emotional growth. People plagued by phobias, compulsions, anxieties, and depressions lack freedom and spontaneity as they try to relate meaningfully to their environment and to other people. Good mental health and a concomitant sense of emotional well-being come from a belief that "I can influence my environment."

If you suffer seriously from any of these death-based emotional problems, you may have to seek help from a professional psychotherapist. But it's also possible to take preventive action now, on your own, while you're still free from these problems or experiencing them only in a mild form.

In our research at Harvard, we've identified a number of general coping strategies which people use to solve various problems and to reduce vulnerability. Some of the strategies are less effective because they bring about a poorer resolution and are less effective in reducing emotional disturbance resulting from these problems.

These less effective strategies include:

1. Withdrawal from people.
2. Avoidance of the problem.
3. Distraction through some activity.
4. Passive, fatalistic acceptance of the problem.
5. Blaming yourself and assuming a heavy load of guilt.
6. Blaming others for your difficulties.

In contrast to these less useful ways of coping, we have found that four other strategies were the most successful in helping people overcome feelings of vulnerability. Here are the more effective ways of coping:

1. *Confront* the problem and take some firm action to resolve it.
2. *Seek additional information* about the problem.
3. *Redefine* the problem so that you can get some perspective on it, or see something favorable in it.
4. *Share your concern* about the problem with other people.

The following chapters are organized to help you apply these four coping strategies as you grapple with the meaning of your own death. Exercises designed to raise your PDA will help you to confront rather than avoid the problem. You will receive additional information about choices and actions that you can take. You may even redefine your sense of death to say, "Dying is not good, but it may not be *that* bad." Finally, as you have a clearer sense that all of us are in this plight together, you'll discover new freedom to talk to others about death and dying.

As these ways of coping help you with the implications of your death, you should begin to undergo a desensitizing process. The more you know about any problem and the more you learn to confront it, the less frightening it becomes. The ultimate goal of this book is to provide you with suggestions that can help you find the healthiest adjustment to your own mortality and aid you in *preventing* some serious death-related emotional disturbances.

---

1. Laura Perls, "One Gestalt Therapist's Approach," in *Life Techniques in Gestalt Therapy*, ed. J. Fagan and I. L. Shepherd (New York: Harper and Row, 1970).

2. Ernest Becker, *The Denial of Death* (New York: Free Press, 1973), 15.
3. Ibid., 57.
4. For an interesting discussion of death and neurosis, see: J.E. Meyer, *Death and Neurosis* (New York: International Universities Press, 1975).
5. Martin E. P. Seligman, *Helplessness* (San Francisco: Freeman, 1976).
6. Ibid.
7. Becker, *op. cit.*, 210.

II

The Death
of
Fear

Chapter Four

BREAKING FREE
FROM FEAR

No sane, healthy person really wants to die. That last appointment is one that almost everyone, no matter how religious, elderly, or bored with life, would like to postpone. The reason that we're so reluctant to confront the end of our existence is not simply that we enjoy life so much. For many of us, it's fear of death and the process of dying that makes us avoid the subject.

You may have drawn happy pictures of death and described it as a warm, welcoming parent in the preceding chapters. Exploring the end of life may also have introduced you to ways of dealing with difficult emotional situations. But in the last analysis, if you look down deep inside yourself, you're still afraid of what death and dying may involve for you personally.

This fear may be partly conscious. But terrors of which we are aware are only a small part of the problem. Elisabeth Kubler-Ross has compared our conscious fears to the tip of a subconscious iceberg which influences our life and attitudes through dreams, art, and bodily and psychological symptoms.

The frightening quality of this subconscious fear of death surfaces in a drawing Dr. Kubler-Ross frequently displays in her lectures. A dying child drew an armored tank with a gun pointing toward a small stick figure of a little boy, who holds a stop sign in his hand but who is helpless to avoid the attack. Through such art, deep-rooted fears make death appear as a catastrophic force bearing down on the individual, leaving him helpless in the path of the onslaught.

Your dreams may also reveal subconscious death fears. A friend of mine recently told me about a dream he had one night after visiting his elderly father. My friend was aware of his father's age and had briefly considered what his father's death would mean to him, but then dismissed the thought from his mind.

In the dream he was sitting in his beachside home. Just offshore he saw a ship which the Navy used for target practice. Suddenly, a hydrogen bomb exploded on the other side of the target ship, and the radioactive fallout began drifting toward his home. He knew he had to get himself and his family out of the area to safety, but he found there was no place to go. The fallout had engulfed everything for miles around. He felt helpless to do anything as this relentless force bore down upon him. Even though his conscious mind could push the challenge of death aside, his unconscious, as manifested in his dream, could not.

In one study of the unconscious fear of death, Dr. Herman Feifel interviewed a group of healthy people who had no reason to believe they would die any time soon, and also a group of terminally ill patients facing imminent death. Using word association tests, he concluded that "patients close to impending death are markedly more afraid of death on an *unconscious* level than healthy individuals." But ironically, Feifel also found a lack of *conscious* fear among the terminally ill. In other words, a person might say he wasn't afraid of death. On a conscious level, he might even believe he had no fear. But his unconscious belied that fact. This high level of unconscious fear, Feifel noted, was independent of the patient's disease, whether cancer or heart trouble. Feifel concluded that "finding little conscious fear of dying in dying individuals, we should not conclude that fear of death is not there. Repudiation of conscious fears may be a way of coping with unconscious anxiety."[1]

Both conscious and unconscious fears can have effects on us. Denying fear on the conscious level can result in an exceptionally low and undesirable Personal Death Awareness, with its attendant lack of freedom. Those who have unconscious terrors submerged in their minds may suffer from anxiety or other psychosomatic manifestations.

Some fears may center on the event of death itself, but many people seem more concerned about the events that lead inexorably to death. "It is not death I fear, but dying," wrote Montaigne. I have talked with many dying patients as well as healthy individuals attending seminars and workshops. The truth of the French essayist's words has struck me over and over again. People fear the dying process as much as death itself. Perhaps this is true of you. Think about it for a minute. Which do you most fear?

_____ I fear death itself more than dying.
_____ I fear dying more than death.

_____ I fear neither.

_____ I fear both of them.

_____ I dislike thinking about either.

If you are in touch with your fears associated with dying as a process, what are they?

The thing which most frightens me about dying is:

_____ the pain.

_____ progressive deterioration and disability.

_____ losing control over personal decisions.

_____ being left alone.

_____ overwhelming emotional feelings.

_____ not knowing what is happening.

_____ being buried before I'm dead.

_____ getting inadequate medical care.

_____ other _____

Now let's explore further some of these fears and see what, if anything, you can do about them.

Fear of Pain. Many people, especially those who have watched relatives suffer the excruciating throes of cancer or another terminal illness, see dying as a painful ordeal. Death is the ultimate injury or illness, and "if a small injury or illness can be painful, there is a certain logic in imagining that the ultimate physical failure must be the ultimate in pain," Robert Neale argues.[2]

Actually, death may occur comfortably and easily, but in a terminal illness, pain does occur often enough to present a valid basis for fear. To eliminate this fear, it's necessary to eliminate the pain. That's usually possible with the pain-killing drugs now available.

There may be two questionable side effects, however. Many of these drugs are addictive, so if you rely on drugs for pain relief, you run this risk. The second side effect is sedation, which can impede your ability to relate to the people around you.

Most American hospitals tend to treat pain very cautiously. For some reason always difficult for me to understand, they don't want their terminal patients to become addicts!

An alternate and more enlightened approach has been taken by St. Christopher's Hospice, a facility for the terminally ill outside London. The St. Christopher's staff have decided they don't want their patients to be preoccupied with pain during their final days. As a result, the physicians ascertain the optimum drug dosage to keep the patient constantly free of pain. One key objective in this treatment is to eliminate even the *anticipation* of pain. Although a person may not be hurting at one stage of treatment, he knows from experience that when his medication wears off, the pain will return. The very anticipation of the onset of the pain results in the patient's preoccupation with the possibility of suffering. Properly applied drug dosages can eliminate this fear. The patient is then free to concentrate on other issues, such as winding up his personal affairs and saying good-bye to family and friends.

The philosophy of medication at St. Christopher's involves keeping the patient pain-free, and at the same time, mentally alert so that he can communicate with others. The staff uses a blend of pain-relieving ingredients including heroin (diamorphine), which is rarely used in the United States. Some of the other morphine derivatives can "zonk" out a patient, or make him less lucid, but heroin has less of a dulling effect on consciousness, even though it is highly addictive.

In sharp contrast to this British approach, a too frequent American approach is illustrated by the experience of a terminal cancer patient named Laura. Preoccupied with a dread of pain, Laura discussed this fear with her physician, who assured her that he would try his best to keep her pain-free. He gave her such a large amount of medication, however, that she was heavily sedated for the major part of her last days. Her wish had been granted, but she was not free to interact with her husband and son, both of whom she had been very close to. A more enlightened approach to drugs might have allowed her both to be pain-free and to have the opportunity to say the necessary good-byes.

How much is the fear of pain a problem for you? If you were forced to make a choice between pain or alertness, which do you think you might choose?

Fear of Loss of Control. You may also be afraid that your dying will involve the loss of personal decisions and an over-dependence on others to do things for you. Such a dying experience might make you feel you've reverted to your childhood, and that can mean a loss of self-esteem. If you become bedridden, certainly you will become more dependent on others.

In the name of love, there is a temptation for the healthier members of a family to try to take over the guidance of the dying person's remaining days. But the result can be the opposite of true love and can in effect strip the sick relative of important self-esteem.

A friend telephoned me one day and said her father was dying of a terminal disease. The father had told the family he wanted to go home to die, but his daughter and the rest of the family were worried about this request because they knew it could mean a shortening of a patient's life.

As I spoke with the daughter, the importance of his need to die at home became clear to me. A carpenter, he had built the house with his own hands. He was distraught with a sense of helplessness because he couldn't override his family's wishes and go home to die. Even though they couldn't see what was happening, he was becoming less of a man every day, less of an individual with a distinctive identity. To him, that house was a symbol of the basic meaning of his entire life, and he was afraid that he would be denied the right to die as he had lived—a proud craftsman in the midst of his handiwork.

Physical impairment doesn't necessarily have to be equated with mental impairment. Dr. Melvin Krant of the Tufts University Medical School in Boston says it's important to permit "a person to stay in control as much as he can, and to feel that loving support which gives him a sense of his own worth, so he can approach death in a courageous and dignified fashion."[3]

I encouraged the carpenter's daughter to let him choose the place where he would die and then, within reason, to do whatever he requested. After some discussion, the family members allowed him to return home, and he died only a few days later. But those were serene, happy days for him because he was settled in familiar surroundings again.

How important would it be to you to retain control over your personal decisions if you found you were dying? If you're afraid you may lose control over your last days of life, think for a moment how you can plan now to maintain some independence, even though you may be confined to a bed. If you let your loved ones know *now* that you want to retain certain powers of decision-making over your life, you may succeed in keeping some control. Try answering the following questions:

When I learn my death is approaching, I would like to have a say about _____

To ensure that I maintain control over this/these area(s) of my life, I could notify _____ about my wishes and enlist his/her support on my behalf. Other ways I can lay the groundwork now for keeping some control over personal decisions are _____

Fear of Physical Disability.   Even if you anticipate maintaining control over personal decisions during your final days, you may be afraid that your life will become onerous or even meaningless through the loss of the use of some part of your body. Dying—especially from a terminal illness—does usually involve an increasing loss of energy, weakening of controls over bodily waste, and an inability to move about as easily as before.

A frequent cause of this impairment is surgery. Surgeons often assume that the most important thing is to extend the patient's life. But patients don't always agree. The *quality* of their remaining months or days may be as important as the length of life. Because of their training and expertise, physicians and surgeons naturally feel that treatment decisions should be left up to them because they think they know what is best for the patient. As far as medical considerations are concerned, they may be right, but other factors make up a happy, satisfied life.

Some physicians say to their patients, "If you undergo surgery, you'll live. If you don't, you'll die." A better approach would be for the doctor to say, "If you undergo this treatment, we can extend your life by approximately this amount and you will have to live with these disabilities. Without treatment, these are the possible consequences. What is your choice?"

The issue was presented in this way to a man in our hospital. He chose *not* to have surgery which would have meant the amputation of his arm and shoulder. He knew the operation would have left him largely immobile in a brace, and would have extended his life only by a year or less. In my opinion, the final choice of whether to undergo an operation resulting in disability should be a joint decision by both doctor and patient. The patient should be kept informed. He should enlist his relatives and friends to pressure doctors to provide him with the facts so that he can exercise his right to choose the level of disability with which he thinks he can live. If the patient makes his own decisions to live or not to live with reduced physical or mental capacities, the fear of disability during the dying process can be lessened considerably.

But it is not always easy to allow the patient to make this kind of decision, because some patients change their minds. I was called into a case where an old gentleman was refusing to have his gangrenous leg removed. He told the nursing staff he wanted to die. He had already had one leg amputated, and he didn't care to live without the other. "I'm an old man," he protested. "I've lived a full life, and now I'm ready to die."

The attending physicians knew if the leg was not removed, the man would die rather quickly, but if the amputation took place, he could conceivably live a number of years. Every fact available, except the old man's attitude, indicated surgery was the proper course of action.

After getting the approval of the man's family, the doctors decided to ignore the patient and remove his leg. I visited him several days after the surgery, and to my surprise he denied ever saying to me or the nursing staff that he had wanted to die. "What do you mean?" he asked. "I never said that. I'm happy to be alive!"

His attitude was similar to a patient who attempts suicide but is rescued. These people sometimes resent being rescued, only to deny several days later that they had any intention of killing themselves.

At this point, consider what level of physical disability you might be willing to live with for an extension of life.

To extend my life, I might be willing to give up the use of:

_____ one arm.

_____ both arms.

_____ one leg.

_____ both legs.

_____ my arms and legs.

_____ a vital organ, such as my heart, which would have to be replaced with a transplant.

_____ my eyes.

_____ my genital organs.

_____ my entire body (complete paralysis).

Author Marya Mannes says she would not want to live as a blind person, and she has stated this desire in a "living will" which she drafted to indicate the circumstances under which she wants to die.[4] I certainly wouldn't want to lose my eyesight either, but I don't think I'd prefer death to living without sight. Many people— Helen Keller is one of the most obvious examples that comes to mind—have lived full, useful lives with this disability. But if I were blind and completely paralyzed, that would be a much harder choice.

Fear of Loneliness. The French philosopher Blaise Pascal said, "We live and die alone; no one can help us." His statement may seem pessimistic, but by its very nature, dying *is* a lonely business. No one else can face your death for you. The fear of dying alone can become especially intense if your relatives and acquaintances begin to avoid you as your death approaches. The tendency to avoid a dying person is not simply a sign of callousness. A natural response in our death-denying, pleasure-oriented culture is to find a convenient excuse not to visit a person who is terminally ill.

A classic study was conducted on the response to call bells in a hospital. A researcher stationed himself in a strategic section of the hospital and recorded the time it took the nursing staff to answer a patient's call light. He found that the sicker and closer to death the patient was, the longer it took the staff to answer the signal.

Many of us avoid the dying because we don't know what to say or how to act around a deathbed. The sick person makes us uncomfortable. He reminds us of our own mortality. The sense of imminent death raises our Personal Death Awareness to an uncomfortable level. If you can overcome this anxiety caused by your

PDA, you can become a key factor in helping dying friends and relatives manage their fear or loneliness. All you have to do is be there. It's not important to have answers to all the questions the ill person asks, because some questions may not have an adequate answer.

Unless you're killed quickly in an accident or are struck down suddenly by a heart attack, you may spend your final days in an incapacitated state, perhaps in a hospital bed. What can you do to protect yourself from the fear of loneliness during your dying hours?

For one thing, you can let your friends and relatives know now, in no uncertain terms, that you want them around when you die. Tell them you won't feel uncomfortable having them beside you, and they shouldn't feel uncomfortable either.

One young student nurse who was dying of a terminal illness found that her hospital friends and fellow nurses were staying away from her hospital room. She used this straightforward approach in a letter to them. "I sense your fright and your fear enhances mine," she wrote. "Why are you afraid? I am the one who is dying! I know you feel insecure, don't know what to say, don't know what to do. But please believe me, if you care, you can't go wrong. Just admit that you care. That is really what we're searching for. We may ask for whys and wherefores, but we don't really expect answers. *Don't run away* . . . wait . . . all I want to know is that there will be someone to hold my hand when I need it. I am afraid. Death may get to be routine for you, but it is new to me. You may not see me as unique, but I have never died before. To me, once is pretty unique!

"You whisper about my youth, but when one is dying, is he really so young any more? I have lots I wish we could talk about. If only we could be honest, . . . admit our fears, touch one another. If you really care, would you lose so much of your valuable professionalism if you even cried with me? Just person to person? Then, it might not be so hard to die . . . in a hospital . . . with friends close by."[5]

If you were suffering from a terminal illness, how would you feel about writing such a letter to a friend? If you would hesitate, is it because of some sense of pride or shyness or for some other reason? I believe it's a mistake not to confront loved ones with how you really feel about loneliness as you're dying. If you resist taking steps to remedy your loneliness, you'll only begin to feel more lonely. Remember that the sense of pride or shyness that seems so important will be meaningless after you're gone.

Fear of Feelings.   You may be afraid that in dying you'll be overcome by intense feelings or emotions that you can't handle. If you have trouble controlling anger, sadness, or depression in your normal everyday living, you're a prime candidate for being fearful of your feelings at death. Perhaps you worry that your displays of emotion will drive the people around you away—especially those assigned to take care of you.

The best way to overcome this fear is to understand that intense feelings are a normal part of the dying process. Does it seem unusual for a dying person to want to cry? Even if the terminally ill patient feels that something better awaits him, he's still likely to be quite unhappy about the impending, permanent separation from friends and loved ones. Tears are appropriate at the death of a loved one, so why shouldn't you cry as your own death approaches?

What emotions do you think you might display at your own death? Which of these emotions are you most afraid of? What do you think would be the most appropriate outlet for your feelings? Elisabeth Kubler-Ross has suggested that every hospital should have a "screaming room," where people can go to shout and yell and express their anger. Dying makes both the patient and his friends want to scream at times, especially when the approaching death seems somehow unjust or unreasonable.

Fear of the Unknown.   No one likes unpleasant surprises, and some people worry that dying will be unpleasant because they won't be informed about what is happening to them. But if you know exactly what is happening to you, you'll probably be more able to detach yourself from the dying process and accept what is occurring in your physical being.

Information is the best antidote for this fear of the unknown. The best way to become informed is to be straightforward and aggressive in demanding facts from your attending physicians. I interviewed a dying man before the medical staff of a Pennsylvania hospital. He described to us what had been helpful in his treatment and what had been useless. One of the things he most appreciated was that the specialist assigned to his case took time to go over medical concepts and treatment procedures with him in great detail.

"I went through the medical literature looking for articles relating to my condition. When I brought those articles to Dr. A., I was really relieved to know that he had read them. It gave me confidence to see he was on top of his field and was sure enough of himself to take the time to discuss the issues with me."

This patient was a teacher who had an especially strong need to gather sufficient facts to solve problems. Because he pushed his doctor for information, he was able to control his fears of the unknown more effectively.

But are there any limits to what a patient should be told about his condition? As a general principle, I believe that patients have a right to know about their diagnosis and prognosis. A refusal to disclose information, or dishonesty with a dying person will inevitably cause feelings of alienation and abandonment.

In our research experience, we've found the best approach for a physician to take is to disclose the seriousness of the disease to the patient in a series of steps adjusted to the patient's own need for information. For example, the doctor might say, "You have a very serious illness." Before proceeding, he can wait for the patient to ask, "How serious?" or "Is it cancer?" The doctor can then disclose additional facts until the patient seems to have enough information to provide comfort for the moment.

This sort of dialogue can be conducted over several sessions to give the dying person time to absorb the details of his condition. We've found that most often, patients desire to know such facts, but for some people, knowing is more important than for others. If a person doesn't want to know anything about his ailment, his desires should be respected. A step-by-step approach can help the physician understand just how much information he should impart.

Without a free exchange of ideas and facts, relationships between the dying person and his family and friends may degenerate into what I call "end games." In the most absurd form of the situation, the patient knows his condition, but doesn't want his family to know because he feels they won't be able to deal with it emotionally. The family also knows everything about the dying person, but they don't think he can hold up through a discussion of the subject. A great deal of energy and valuable time can be wasted through conspiracies of silence and ploys to avoid conversation. Usually one side or the other gets frustrated with these games and finally breaks the silence. The result is a great sense of relief all around.

Fear of Being Buried Alive.   This fear may seem somewhat bizarre, but it's surprising how many people worry that they will be pronounced dead while only unconscious and then wake up several feet underground. Occasional stories about how the inside of some exhumed coffins show fingernail scratches enhance this fear.

After a lecture I delivered in the West, a very alert ninety-year-old woman sent word through her daughter that she wanted to speak with me after the meeting. "You know, Dr. Worden, I believe God will take care of me after I die. I'm not really afraid of death. But there's something else that bothers me. You'll probably think this is silly, but I'm afraid people might think I'm dead and then bury me alive. I think I'd go crazy if I woke up and found myself underground, with no choice but to suffocate. I've never told anyone else about this, and I try not to even think about it."

It had obviously been hard for her to disclose these feelings to me. I thought for a moment and then asked, "Do you have any close relatives?"

"Yes, my daughter is here at this meeting. She lives near me."

"Have you told her about your fear?"

"No." She shook her head. "I didn't see any reason to burden her with my worries."

"Well," I replied, "I think you should tell her. Let her know how much this thought of being buried alive bothers you. Ask her to be sure that when you die, she'll check with the doctors to be sure you're really dead."

"Yes, that might be a good idea."

"Also," I continued, "get in touch with your physician and tell him about this concern. If you explain it in the same way you explained it to me, he'll know how important it is to you. This is quite a common fear, you know, and as a practical matter, most people are definitely dead when they're buried because they've been embalmed. But your doctor has probably had other people mention this to him. Ask him to double-check and be certain that you really are dead when he examines your body."

"I don't know why I didn't think of that!" she said, smiling now. "That makes me feel so much better."

The knowledge that she could *do* something about her fear helped this woman manage her feelings better and put her attitude toward death in a healthier perspective. Her religious faith had given her an assurance of a life after death and had provided her with the basis for a healthy Personal Death Awareness. But her fear of being buried alive had induced her to deny death on another level and to refuse to discuss her misgivings with relatives or even think about logical solutions to her fear. Her courage and willingness to bring the subject up with me, a stranger, had provided her with a means to raise her Personal Death Awareness to a more acceptable level. As a result, she found relief from her fear through exercising some control over the dying process.

One or more of these fears of dying usually plague healthy people and those who have just entered the dying process. Those who are closer to the end may be free of fear. "Fear of dying and of death may be more typical of early stages than of the later phases of incurable illness," observes Dr. Avery Weisman. "As time passes, people become more accepting of limitations, so that when death approaches, it is not always accompanied by growing fears."[6] But there's no sense in waiting for this natural and gradual lessening of anxiety to take over just before you die. You can do something about it now:

1. *Look your fear straight in the eye.*   Don't be afraid to think about your fear and search for a solution. Fears are usually the flip side of things that we wish or hope for. For example, if you want to have a lot of friends, you're likely to be afraid of *not* having any as you die; you dread being lonely. You've already indicated what you fear about dying, but think about your personal fears once again. Are they the same fears that you had at the beginning of this chapter? Indicate your two greatest fears below:

My greatest fear in dying is _____

My second greatest fear is _____

2. *Speak to your family or friends about your fear.* This may make you self-conscious, but it can make an interesting topic of conversation. Ask people about their own feelings first: "What do you fear most about dying?" Then tell them what your own fears are. Finally, try to help each other come up with some possible solutions to help manage these fears.

Be sure to discuss this matter with the people who will have the most influence with your doctors as you face the dying process. If there are certain choices you want to be able to make right up to the end, let your loved ones know and encourage them to help you fulfill your wishes. By discussing your desires in advance, you'll make it easier for people to discuss these same subjects in your presence while you're on your deathbed. They'll feel more comfortable around you and won't be as likely to look for excuses to avoid your hospital room or put up a pretense. As for myself, I hope my family won't feel obliged to gush, "Oh, how well you look!" or, "You'll be out of that bed in no time!" That kind of phoniness might encourage me to postpone choices and decisions I should be making and reduce our opportunity for deep, meaningful communications about my approaching death.

3. *Check out your physician.* Find out what his philosophy of pain management is. If it doesn't suit you, shop around until you find a doctor whose views coincide with your own.

The next time you go in for a checkup, bring up the subject of your death. If your doctor tries to shrug off the subject by saying, "Oh, you're too healthy to worry about that," push him and let him know how serious you are. If he still wants to talk about something else, his own Personal Death Awareness may be too low, because of his own denial of death, for him to help you properly.

When you find a receptive physician, let him know how you feel about physical disability, about the prolonging of life, and about making certain decisions up to the end. There seems to be an increasing tendency for those who think seriously about how they want to die to take the initiative well ahead of time with their doctors. After speaking at a large conference of retired persons in the South, I was amazed to learn how many of those in attendance had discussed their preferences with their physicians.

It's advisable to tell the doctor in advance how you'd like to be informed if you have cancer or some other terminal illness. If you change your mind later, you'll at least put him on notice that you've thought the issue through, and he'll be more likely to follow your instructions. Even if your family physician isn't in charge of your case, he'll be in a position to see that the specialists assigned to you will carry out your wishes. Medicine is a close fraternity, and physicians listen to and respect one another.

These three approaches to reducing your fears of dying are by no means the only methods available to you, but they can help. Take a moment to think how you can apply these ideas in minimizing the forces that frighten you about dying.

MY PLAN

You can't hold back death itself. Each of us has to keep that final appointment, and that's certainly a cause for some uncertainty, nervousness, and healthy fear. But it's a well-known psychological principle that a sense of helplessness aggravates fear. If you realize that you can affect your environment and the factors that cause you to be afraid, the intensity of your fears will diminish. You can find relief from many of your fears of dying if you tackle those fears head-on.

1. Herman Feifel, J. Freilich, and L. J. Hermann, "Death Fear in Dying Heart and Cancer Patients," *J. Psychosom. Res.*, 17(1973), 161-166.
2. Robert Neale, *The Art of Dying* (New York: Harper and Row, 1973).
3. Melvin Krant, "The Doctor, Fatal Illness, and the Family," in *Concerning Death: A Practical Guide for the Living*, ed. E. A. Grollman (Boston: Beacon Press, 1974).
4. Marya Mannes, *Last Rights* (New York: William Morrow and Co., Inc., 1973).
5. B. M. Mount, "Death—A Part of Life," *Crux*, 11 (1973-1974), 5.
6. Avery D. Weisman, *On Dying and Denying: A Psychiatric Study of Terminality* (New York: Behavioral Publications, 1972).

Chapter Five

FREEDOM THROUGH FAITH

Death has always played a leading role in Western religion because it poses the ultimate questions: Who are we? Where did we come from? Where are we going?

The Apostle Paul, echoing the prophet Hosea, sounds a note of triumph: "O death, where is thy sting? O grave, where is thy victory?"

These words have become a rallying cry for Western religious thought: the fear of death—not just of dying, but death itself and all the anxieties rooted in the dread of nonexistence—can be overcome by faith.[1]

Some of the best-known passages of the Bible concern death. The twenty-third Psalm, familiar to most people and often used at both Jewish and Christian funeral services, indicates the resources which faith offers to those facing death. Here are excerpts from this Psalm taken from the Scottish Psalter of 1650:

> Yea, though I walk through death's dark vale,
> Yet will I fear no ill;
> For Thou art with me and Thy rod
> And staff me comfort still.
>
> Goodness and mercy all my life
> Shall surely follow me;
> And in God's house forevermore
> My dwelling place shall be.

This Psalm gives the believer a source of strength in dying ("for Thou art with me") and also a sense of what comes after death ("and in God's house my dwelling place shall be").

Just how well do these comforting words work out in practice? Are believers more likely to face the end of life in a peaceful, assured frame of mind than nonbelievers?

Begin to answer these questions by taking a look at yourself. Examine your own religious commitment, and its possible relationship to your fear of death.

I consider myself:

_____ a very religious person.
_____ a moderately religious person.
_____ a slightly religious person.
_____ not religious at all.

Now rate yourself on the following fear-of-death scale which was developed by psychologist David Lester.[2]

agree	not sure	disagree	
_____	_____	_____	1. I would avoid death at all costs.
_____	_____	_____	2. The total isolation of death frightens me.
_____	_____	_____	3. I am disturbed by the physical degeneration involved in a slow death.
_____	_____	_____	4. I would not mind dying young.
_____	_____	_____	5. Dying might be an interesting experience.
_____	_____	_____	6. I view death as a release from earthly suffering.
_____	_____	_____	7. The pain involved in dying frightens me.
_____	_____	_____	8. I am disturbed by the shortness of life.
_____	_____	_____	9. The feeling that I might be missing out on so much after I die bothers me.
_____	_____	_____	10. The fact that I don't know what it feels like to be dead doesn't bother me.
_____	_____	_____	11. If I had a fatal disease, I would like to be told.
_____	_____	_____	12. The idea of never thinking or experiencing again after I die does not bother me.
_____	_____	_____	13. I am not disturbed by death being the end of life as I know it.
_____	_____	_____	14. The intellectual degeneration of old age disturbs me.
_____	_____	_____	15. I am disturbed by the thought that my abilities will be limited while I lie dying.

Give yourself one point for each statement that you *agreed* with from lines 1, 2, 3, 7, 8, 9, 14, and 15, and put your total in Box I. Now give yourself one point for each statement you *disagreed* with from lines 4, 5, 6, 10, 11, 12, and 13, and insert this total in Box II. Finally, add the scores in Boxes I and II and put this grand total in Box III.

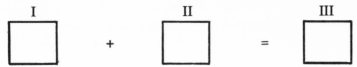

I   +   II   =   III

If you scored 1-5 in Box III, you have a low fear-of-death level. If you scored 6-10, your fear-of-death rating is in the medium range. If you scored 11-15, you are extremely afraid of death and dying. Now compare your fear-of-death rating with your religious commitment. If you consider yourself religious, do you find you have a correspondingly low fear of death? The answers to this question may be different from what you would expect.

Several studies have been conducted on the relationship of religion to fear of death, but they have provided little in the way of conclusive evidence. One of the more comprehensive investigations was done by Herman Feifel, author of *The Meaning of Death*. In studying the impact of religious persuasion on death fear in a group of healthy people and also a group of terminally ill patients, he found no difference between believers and non-believers in the intensity of conscious fear.[3]

My own observation of dying patients suggests that religious persons can find great resources to help them in their dying. But for some, religion can actually get in the way. It's not so much whether you are religious, but rather the degree to which your religious beliefs are integrated into your life.

Elisabeth Kubler-Ross confirms this conclusion: "Intensely religious people accept death more easily than most others ... if they are authentic and have internalized their faith. The significant variable is not what you believe but how truly and genuinely you believe. Truly religious people with a deep abiding relationship with God have found it much easier to face death with equanimity."[4]

The limitations of a merely nominal faith came out in a study John Hinton conducted in Great Britain. He found that "those who had a firm religious faith and attend their church ... frequently were most free from anxiety. The next ... group, [who] professed faith but made little outward observance of it, were more anxious to a significant extent.[5]

Aside from the intensity and authenticity of religious belief, there may be still another limitation on faith as an antidote to fear of death. In a presentation at a New York thanatology conference, the Reverend David Read suggested that religion is beneficial to those who believe in God's grace and mercy and trust that their relationship with God will continue into the afterlife.[6] Read argued, however, that those who adhere rigidly to church rules and practices may feel cheated at death and are likely to suffer anxiety. Apparently, they sense that God is letting them down at death by failing to bestow favors such as a longer life, which they feel He "owes" them for their strict devotion.

Integrated religious belief which can bring the "victory" over death that the Apostle Paul acclaims is illustrated by Martha, an eighty-year-old woman. Even though she had undergone multiple surgeries and had been in pain for years, she had a deep and abiding faith which sustained her right up to the end.

When the pain was at its worst, she couldn't get to sleep, and it was then that Martha would rely most heavily on God. She prayed constantly, but her supplications weren't just for herself. As she put it, she would "go around the world" in her prayers for the hundreds of people who were on her "prayer list." Many of those whom she asked God to guide were young people who had become so impressed with the depth of her spirituality that they visited her on a regular basis. She had no living relatives, so it meant a great deal to her to be able to share her convictions with these young people whom she considered her extended family.

"Aren't you afraid of dying?" I asked her.

"No, not really," she replied. "I am grateful that I know Him and one day I will be with Him."

Many elderly people in Martha's condition begin to regress and deteriorate. They let others care for them and make no effort to reach out and help those around them. But Martha never lost her concern for others, either in the hospital or in the nursing home where she lived when not undergoing treatment. When a young friend or a nurse gave her something—any small thing like a card, a picture, or some other inexpensive item—she always was very grateful. She had extremely few material goods, but she valued the gifts she received as concrete symbols of her relationship with her many friends.

Martha was not an elderly Pollyanna, however, who could only see the bright side of things. She became quite discouraged at times, and as her death drew nearer, she said to me on several occasions, "I'm so tired, I wish He would take me." Her profound faith allowed her to see a purpose in her suffering. She gained perspective on her condition by referring to the pain experienced by Christ and Christian saints like Paul.

Martha's love for others continued to have an impact even after the last thread of her fragile life snapped. She arranged to show her love and concern by donating her body to research because of her unusual medical history. And several hundred of her "family," who had visited her frequently in her final days, came together one last time to pay her homage at a memorial service. Her faith, as an integral part of her very being, had helped her through dying just as it had helped her through life.

Martha was a classic example of what Elisabeth Kubler-Ross has called an "authentic" and "internalized" faith, which knows little fear of death. But for every Martha, whose faith sustains, there is a Frank, whose religion gives problems in dying.

Frank was born and reared in a very strict religious home. As a boy, he had even thought about the ministry. When he reached his mid-twenties, his religious habits changed. He attended occasional services, gave lip service to certain doctrines, but lived as he pleased and didn't bother to make religion a part of his life.

When he reached his mid-forties, Frank learned that he had cancer. Feeling he had not taken the religious training of his youth seriously enough, he was struck with a sense of guilt. "I know I'm not good enough to go to heaven," he told our hospital chaplain who tried to console him. "With my past life, there's no way I'm going to get there."

"God is more interested in what you believe and do *now* than what you've done in the past," the chaplain said reassuringly. "Our God is a forgiving God of mercy who knows that no one, on his own merits, is good enough to have eternal life."

Frank refused to believe that. In desperation, he tried to salvage the religion he had taken so lightly during the past twenty years. He constantly reviewed his past life, the mistakes and sins he felt he had committed. But the more he dwelt on them, the more certain he became that God would have nothing to do with him. "My illness and death are the punishment God is handing me for not following him," Frank told the chaplain.

"God doesn't operate like that," the minister protested, but Frank refused to listen. He read the Scriptures, asked forgiveness of people he thought he had wronged, and cast about for any other penances he could imagine. But none of these attempts worked; he could not cram twenty years of religion into his few remaining months of life. Since his religion did not have a clear meaning to him, he died a fearful, unhappy man. He would have been more comfortable in his dying if he had not been religious at all. Faith for him was not really faith, providing support and comfort, but a specter from his youth which rose to haunt him.

Martha and Frank illustrate the impact of religious faith on the fear of death: the *quality* of your religion is the key factor. An important study supporting this was done by Raymond Carey at the Lutheran General Hospital in suburban Chicago. Carey's team studied eighty-four incurably ill patients who were expected to die within a year. The investigators, focusing on how patients coped emotionally with their limited life expectancy, examined the role religion played in the dying process.

Carey separated the patients into *intrinsically religious* and *extrinsically religious* people. The intrinsically religious person, according to Carey's criteria, lives the teachings of his faith. He takes seriously the commandment of brotherhood, strives to transcend selfish needs, and tempers rigid dogma with loving humility. In contrast, the extrinsically religious patient takes a self-determined approach to life and focuses on his own personal safety, social standing, and narrow interests. This person uses religion to bargain his way into heaven instead of trying to live his faith in any serious sense.

After studying these two types of religious personalities, Carey concluded that "the most important aspect of the religious variable was the quality of the religious orientation, rather than mere religious affiliation or verbal acceptance of religious beliefs. Those who had tried to integrate their beliefs into their life-style had the greatest emotional adjustment to dying."[7]

What about your own religious beliefs and death? Take a minute to consider what you believe at this point in time.

1. My personal religious beliefs and practices include:
   _____ a. Faith in a deity who is concerned about me as an individual.

_____ b. Personal prayer or meditation several times a week.

_____ c. Regular reading of religious literature (the Bible, inspirational books, devotionals, etc.).

_____ d. Regular church or synagogue attendance (at least twice a month).

_____ e. Confidence that God can guide me in my career and family life.

_____ f. Regular efforts to relate to other people in a moral way that is consistent with my faith.

_____ g. An ability to draw strength from my faith when things are going wrong.

2. What I believe about God and my death:

_____ a. God is interested in my death.

_____ b. God is not interested in my death.

_____ c. I hope God is interested in my death.

_____ d. I'm not sure whether there is a God.

_____ e. I don't believe there is a God.

_____ f. Other: _____

3. What I believe about an afterlife:

_____ a. I believe there is a heaven, and I'm sure I'll go there.

_____ b. I'm not sure, but I hope there is a life after death.

_____ c. I'm not interested in the subject.

_____ d. I am quite sure there is no afterlife. When you're dead, you're dead.

_____ e. Other: _____

4. My concept of what happens after death is: _____
_____

5. What I'm counting on to get me through the dying process is:
_____

Obviously, there are a variety of possible answers, but your responses can give you some indication of the intensity of your religious commitment. For example, if you checked three or more of the items in question one, you're probably more serious than most people about your faith. If you could also honestly check the "a" answers in questions 2 and 3, you have a good foundation for convictions that can support you through the dying process. But only you know the actual authenticity and depth of your beliefs— the inner quality that will determine how you fare in the end.

So far we have concentrated on the way religious people confront death. But what about the nonbeliever, the agnostic, the skeptic? According to some current research, the number of people who fall into the nonreligious category may be on the rise. From his British investigations, John Hinton has concluded that "increasingly few, it seems, are protected from the fear of death by the belief that it is not an annihilation, but the beginning of a fuller life."[8] More specifically, Belgian sociologist Pierre Delooz determined from a worldwide study that the belief in an afterlife has been decreasing during the past twenty-five years.[9]

Is there any chance these nonbelievers can die calmly and peacefully? Or are they doomed to anxiety, fear, and remorse during their last minutes of life?

Studies of fear in nonbelievers are even sketchier than those of fear in believers. But those who work with dying patients testify that some without faith are able to confront the end as comfortably and serenely as certain types of religious people. I myself was brought up hearing sermons that believers experience peaceful deaths and nonbelievers usually are wracked by anguish. After working with many dying patients, I've been amazed at how well some nonreligious people die. Elisabeth Kubler-Ross has come to a similar conclusion: "I have found that true atheists have died with amazing peace and acceptance no different from a religious person."[10]

Robert Kavanaugh, a former priest, makes a similar observation in his book, *Facing Death.*[11] "Skeptics and agnostics can find peace at the end, plus assurance of safety in any possible hereafter, if their search is their creed and they are sincerely committed to it," he writes. "When any quest for truth is real, not mere talk or laziness, not indifference or being too busy, it can reward the searcher with all the wealth found in true belief."

One explanation for the ability of some nonreligious people to meet death bravely may be that, in a deep philosophical sense, they have become comfortable with the idea that death is inevitable and must be faced and accepted. The existential philosophy of Martin Heidegger and Sartre has influenced many, even some who don't know what Existentialism is. This philosophy sees death as the end—a move into nothingness. But the theme of nothingness, according to Paul Irion, "does not imply that death is of no consequence. The acceptance of death as natural and the definition in terms of nothingness do not cancel each other out. In facing the nothingness of death man may be able to live his remaining days with authenticity."[12]

But many people who have discarded their religious beliefs have not affirmed any coherent alternative philosophy such as Existentialism. Instead of trying seriously to answer the ultimate questions about the meaning of death, they choose to postpone or ignore the issue. Perhaps this is true of you. If so, let me encourage you not to ignore these big questions. By developing a deep and certain philosophy of life, you will have not only important resources to help you die, but also resources to help you with the cares and hassles that each of us face every day.

1. I Cor. 15:55
2. David Lester, personal communication. This scale is a modification of Lester's original scale.
3. Herman Feifel, "Religious Conviction and Fear of Death Among the Healthy and the Terminally Ill," *Journal for the Scientific Study of Religion,* 13 (1974), 353-360.
4. Elisabeth Kubler-Ross, *Questions and Answers on Death and Dying* (New York: Macmillan Publishing Co., Inc., 1974).
5. John Hinton, *Dying* (Baltimore, Maryland: Penguin Books Inc., 1967).
6. David H. C. Read, "The Concept of God of the Terminally Ill." Position paper from Thanatology Workshop, Foundation of Thanatology, November 4, 1972, New York City.
7. Raymond G. Carey, *Living Until Death* (Park Ridge, Illinois, Lutheran General Hospital, 1974).
8. John Hinton, *Dying* (Baltimore, Maryland: Penguin Books Inc., 1967).
9. Pierre Delooz, "Who Believes in the Hereafter?" in *Death and Presence; The Psychology of Death and the After-Life* (Studies in the Psychology of Religion, Vol. 5), ed. A. Godin (Brussels, Belgium: Lumen Vitae Press, 1972).
10. Elisabeth Kubler-Ross, *Questions and Answers on Death and Dying* (New York: Macmillan Publishing Co., Inc., 1974).
11. Robert E. Kavanaugh, *Facing Death* (Los Angeles: Nash Publishing Corporation, 1972).
12. Paul Irion, "The Agnostic and the Religious—Their Coping With Death." Position paper from Thanatology Workshop, Foundation of Thanatology, November 4, 1972, New York City.

Chapter Six

FLYING OVER THE BOUNDARY

One day, a teen-ager who was dying with chronic kidney disease said to me, "Dying is such a drag!" She didn't mean that she was in terrible physical pain. She was referring to the emotional anguish, frustration, and lack of meaning that often accompany the knowledge that you only have a few months to go.

Ted Rosenthal, a young poet with leukemia, echoed my teen-aged friend's sentiments when he declared, "I'm sick of dying. I tell you it's a waste of time. It makes me depressed."[1]

Terminally ill patients inevitably have times of extremely high Personal Death Awareness. Sometimes they become so preoccupied with their own deaths that severe depression or anxiety sets in. Some people can lower their PDA and mitigate their mental suffering by finding meaning in relationships or in a deep religious faith. But for those who don't find solace in these resources, other approaches are available to counter the psychological pain of dying. If you know about these options now, you can have resources to relieve depression and anxiety should your religious faith and other personal resources need assistance during the dying process.

One of the most controversial of these treatments involves the use of psychedelic drugs like LSD. A great deal of suspicion has surrounded LSD because of the popularity of the drug among youthful members of the hippie counterculture during the 1960s. More recently, accusations have been made that LSD was improperly administered to members of the United States Armed Forces and to other government employees and was responsible for mental disturbances and even death.

Not all applications of psychedelic drugs have resulted in negative reactions, however. Therapeutic use of LSD was begun in earnest in the 1960s with alcoholic and schizophrenic patients. These patients reported after the treatment that they experienced "a sense of increased personal integration, loss of anxiety and depression, and a feeling of inner peace."[2]

One of the earliest attempts to use LSD with dying patients occurred in 1960 during some experiments by Dr. Eric Kast, a Chicago physician particularly interested in the drug's pain-relieving properties. Although Dr. Kast did little to prepare his patients for their high-flying "trips," he did observe and report some of the hallucinogenic effects: "In addition to pain relief, these patients displayed a peculiar disregard for the gravity of their situation. [They] talked freely about their impending death with an affect considered inappropriate in our western civilization but most beneficial to their own psychic states."[3]

The promise of a potion that could produce a worry-free death must have been exciting to early researchers like Kast. A more systematic study of the possibilities of psychedelic drugs with dying patients began almost by accident in 1965 at Maryland's Spring Grove State Hospital, later renamed the Maryland State Psychiatric Research Center. A female researcher in her forties discovered she had terminal cancer, which was becoming more and more painful. She decided she needed the external, mood-elevating support that LSD could give her, so she asked her co-workers to let her try the drug. The Spring Grove work with dying patients had begun.

Unlike many of the negative reports in the popular press of LSD effects, this woman experienced a sense of peace and philosophical calm that bordered on religious insight: "I was alone in a timeless world with no boundaries," she said during the experience. "There was no atmosphere, there was no color, no imagery. Suddenly, I recognized that I was a moment in time. ... Again in the void, alone without the time-space boundaries. Life reduced itself over and over again to the least common denominator. I became poignantly aware that the core of life is love. ... At this moment I felt that I was reaching out to the world—to all people—but especially to those closest to me. I wept long for the wasted years, the search for identity in false places, the neglected opportunities, the emotional energy lost in basically meaningless pursuits."

A sense of ultimate meaning and peace remained as the effects of the drug wore off. "I felt joy, not only for myself but for having been able to [make] use [of] the experience of these people [the treatment team]," she said in describing the final phase of the treatment. "Later, as members of my family came, there was a closeness that seemed new. I was radiant, they said. I seemed at peace. ... Some of my physical symptoms were gone ... the excessive fatigue, some of the pain."[4]

Five weeks after her LSD trip, this female researcher died. But she had paved the way for more extensive research on dying patients under the leadership of my friend, Dr. Walter Pahnke. After Dr. Pahnke's untimely death in 1971, the work of the Spring Grove team continued uninterrupted under the leadership of Dr. Stanislav Grof. They have established a comprehensive alternative approach to relieving the emotional suffering of people who are terminally ill.

How would you feel about taking a hallucinogenic drug like LSD if you found you were going to die soon? Try putting a finger on your feelings and note your reaction below:

_____ LSD therapy appeals to me, and I would have little hesitancy in asking for it.

_____ I don't believe in taking LSD or other such drugs.

_____ I'm afraid of psychedelic drugs because we don't know enough about them.

_____ I don't think I will need drug therapy because I'm strong enough in other ways to be able to overcome emotional anguish at death.

_____ This drug therapy sounds interesting, but I'd like to know more about it.

Most negative reactions to LSD therapy result from a lack of knowledge about exactly how the treatment works. The best way to overcome this lack is for you to experience—at least secondhand—an actual LSD session. Imagine that you've been experiencing pain, and your doctors finally diagnose your problem as terminal pancreatic cancer. You only have about six months to live. Finding that your personal resources are not sufficient to keep your spirits up, you fall into a deep depression.

Despite an overwhelmingly gloomy frame of mind, you recall you've heard somewhere about the experiments of the Maryland Center, so you ask your doctor to check into this possibility. Word comes back from the Center that they're interested in you.

You and other prospective patients go through a screening process, which requires you to pass the following test:

1. You must be experiencing some degree of physical pain, depression, anxiety, or psychological isolation. With your pain and depression, you qualify here.
2. You must have a life expectancy of three months. This is true in your case.
3. There should be no brain impairment. You qualify.
4. There should be no gross psychiatric impairment. Your depression is serious, but not so serious that you're regarded as a borderline psychotic.

After you've passed these tests, the research team discusses with you and your family all the procedures and the possible benefits—as well as the risks—involved in drug therapy. Your spouse seems a little wary because he or she still associates LSD with the excesses of the hippie movement, but you are actually becoming enthusiastic. You know how miserably depressed you've been feeling, and you can also see that there's a possibility you'll be contributing something to medical research. Besides, the anticipation of embarking on this last adventure of your life has given you a sense of meaning and direction that has already relieved your depression to some extent. Finally, a family consensus is reached, and you sign the consent form that will launch you on your final, psychedelic trip.

There are three parts to your treatment[5] which might be designated the takeoff, the flight itself, and the landing.

1. *The takeoff.*   The first part of your treatment consists of a series of drug-free interviews covering a period of ten to twelve hours. The therapist assigned to you will learn about your past and your "psychodynamics," or why you do or do not do certain things. He will probe the situations and incidents you consider to be particularly difficult in your life and the defenses you have developed to cope with your anxiety and depression.

After the therapist learns something about what makes you tick, he'll give you an extensive "preflight" briefing on exactly what will happen after you take LSD. He'll also answer any questions you may have. During these conversations, you and the therapist hope to build up a trust relationship which will be important to the success of your drug experience.

2. *The flight.*   When the therapist believes that the first stage has been successfully completed, and you're ready to proceed, the

two of you will set up a time for the administering of the drug. On the day you pick, a specially trained nurse will prepare your room with pictures, flowers, and other objects of your choosing. She will also give you some eyeshades to cut out any visual distractions and stereophonic headphones so that you can listen to music. Musical accompaniment has been found effective in helping a patient let go of his usual psychological defenses and in enhancing emotional awareness in general.

As you sit there wearing your "flight gear," you may feel like some astronaut who is poised on a launching pad, ready to blast off and explore a strange new world. You'll then take the drug—usually injected into a muscle—and your mind will soon begin to alter its ordinary everyday consciousness. Your therapists, including a doctor and a nurse, will be at your side constantly for the ten- to twelve-hour session. They'll observe your body posture and any comments you make. You'll be encouraged to delve into your hallucinogenic experience, but you won't be pressed to give a blow-by-blow account unless you want to. The therapists will interfere as little as possible so that you can enjoy the experience to the fullest.

If you encounter something frightening, your therapist will encourage you to confront it squarely and work your way through it until you come to some resolution. At this stage, the doctor or nurse may alter the music to complement the deep inner problems you're wrestling with. If your mind is passing through a more tranquil and serene phase, the music can again be changed—perhaps to something like Debussy's *La Mer*—to enhance your sense of peace. In these highly controlled sessions, the therapists are quite sensitive to what you're going through because they themselves have undergone LSD experiences as part of their own training.

As you begin to descend from your drug high at the end of the day, your close family members will be brought to your side to be with you. The Spring Grove staff has found that this meeting at the end of the session has often resulted in significant emotional exchanges between patients and their families.

3. *The landing.* The third phase of your treatment will start the next day, as you and your therapist begin a series of interviews aimed at helping you integrate your new insights and feelings

about yourself. The therapist will ask you to write out or dictate a report of your experiences on your drug trip. Although each experience is unique, you may be interested in this account of what one forty-two-year-old woman felt on her LSD "flight":[6]

She became depressed after she underwent a hysterectomy for cancer. Even though her husband constantly reassured her of his love, she felt sexually unacceptable. She was also quite anxious about her older son's plans to marry a girl she didn't like and about a personality conflict she was having with an elderly aunt. Finally, her younger son's sexual development bothered her.

Immediately after she was given LSD, she complained of nausea and cried, "How can anyone expect me to hold it all in?" Then she vomited. The therapists saw this sickness as not only a loss of food, but as an expulsion of repressed feelings. Soon after the nausea left her, she began to focus on her husband and found she was able to solve the problems in that relationship and accept his concern for her: "Darling, you have been everything to me, lover, father, everything," she said. "How could you be all those things to me? We have been genuine to each other. I want you there with me to the end."

The drug then induced her to dwell on her sons. She decided that she could accept her older son's choice of wife, and she also faced up to her unspoken fear about her younger son's sexual identity. As she overcame her anxieties about each of the young men, she had visions of a beautiful emerald on a velvet pillow. Her thoughts then returned to her transformed relationship with her husband, and the vision of the emerald reappeared. But this time she felt pulled into the sparkling beauty of the stone and toward a more meaningful kind of life.[7]

"I've made my peace with God," she declared as she emerged from her LSD trip. "Each man has to make his own. . . . I've had many wonderful things happen. It's got to all work out. I've made it with my Maker! They can do whatever they want over my body. Life has been beautiful, even though painful and hard. It's been beautiful."

After she had completed the experience and her family members had gathered around her, she found that her interactions with them were more loving and genuine. Much of the hostility she had felt toward the elderly aunt was gone. She affirmed her faith in her younger son. She told her older son that she was sorry his fiancée couldn't be present at her bedside and looked forward to welcoming her into the family.

About a week later, she was discharged to her home and reported "a decrease in the severity of . . . pain, an increase in . . . general energy level, and continued reduction of depression and anxiety." Eight months after her LSD trip she was readmitted to the hospital because of severe pain, and two weeks later she died. But even in those last days, she recalled the vision of the emerald as she talked with her therapist and "seemed to derive a sense of meaning and serenity from the memory, even in the midst of her pain."[8]

In an effort to reach some generalizations about the effect of LSD therapy on dying patients, the research team at the Maryland Center measured the reactions to the drug by a number of standards, such as intensity of pain and its effect on certain personality characteristics. When these standards were applied to a group of forty-one patients, the researchers found that thirteen showed dramatic improvement after their psychedelic experiences, thirteen improved moderately, and seven remained unchanged. Only three patients displayed any decline in emotional well-being after the LSD, and most of this decline was slight.[9]

Like the female patient with her vision of an emerald, most dramatic changes seem to follow an "intense psychedelic 'peak experience'—an experience of cosmic unity, usually preceded by . . . agony, death, and spiritual rebirth," Dr. Albert Kurland observed. "Profound experiences of this kind were observed in approximately twenty-five percent of the psychedelic sessions of the cancer patients."[10]

The reason that drugs like LSD ease the psychological anguish— the depressions and anxieties—of dying seems related to the way that the drugs enhance a sense of death's ultimate meaning. "Death, instead of being seen as the end of everything and a step into nothingness, appears suddenly as a transition into a different type of existence for those who undergo the destruction-rebirth-cosmic-unity experience," Dr. Stanislav Grof explained. "The idea of possible continuity of consciousness beyond physical death becomes much more plausible than the opposite. The patients who have transcendental experiences develop a rather deep belief in the ultimate cosmic unity of all creation and experience themselves as part of it without regard to the situation they are facing."[11] Despite this hopeful attitude of many LSD patients, however, Grof adds one word of caution: "Whether these are valid insights into the nature of reality, or merely merciful delusions, I don't think we can say for certain."

As experiments with drugs have expanded, hallucinogenic substances other than LSD have also been used in treatment. One drug called DPT has an effect similar to LSD, but the trip it produces is much shorter—only about four or five hours, as opposed to ten to twelve hours.

Although this psychedelic therapy has a number of ardent supporters, many death researchers remain wary about relying too heavily on drugs, and not enough on warm personal relationships in treating the depressions and anxieties of terminally ill patients. "If together with adequate physical care, the dying person had sufficient human companionship, most of his anguish would be prevented," declares Dr. John Hinton.[12] Dr. Elisabeth Kubler-Ross agrees with this stress on supportive relationships when she warns, "Psychopharmacologic agents should always and only be used as adjunct therapy and not as substitutes for human care."[13]

Some opponents of drug therapy also argue that "dying high" precludes the possibility of suffering and the inner growth that suffering can offer an individual. In my experience, most people who advocate the redemptive benefits of suffering aren't speaking out of a suffering existence. Instead these scholars usually write from their libraries or studies where, at the onset of a headache, they reach for the nearest aspirin bottle.

Hallucinogenic drugs are not the only aids which can help you fly over the last boundary of life. You also can choose a second alternative—hypnosis.

Hypnosis has often been surrounded by a sensational mystique because of its use on the stage, but it's relatively straightforward. It enables you to concentrate better and opens your mind to suggestions that can improve your emotional well-being. In your everyday life, you have the capacity to become absorbed in a train of thought to the exclusion of everything around you. Hypnosis exploits this faculty for becoming totally engrossed by helping you focus on an appropriate thought as you sink into a state of deep relaxation. I've used hypnotism extensively in my own clinical work and have found it an invaluable aid for resolving a number of psychological problems.

Hypnosis can be especially helpful in controlling some type of pain. Most pain has both a biological and psychological component. The better you can handle the psychological dimension, especially the anticipation, the more comfortable you'll become, and the pain will seem less intense. If you can reduce pain through hypnosis, you require less pain medication with its frequent side effects—especially grogginess and fuzzy thinking.

The experience of Louise illustrates the advantages of hypnosis. A thirty-seven-year-old housewife with four children, she was dying and had been in a stupor for three weeks because of massive doses of narcotics. The drugs helped her severe pain and tendency to become nauseous, and they allowed her to sleep. But she resented the grogginess which made it impossible for her to spend her few remaining days in meaningful contact with her family. When her physician suggested that hypnosis might be an alternate solution, she readily agreed.

On the day of her hypnosis session she went off drugs, and a therapist helped her go into a trance for several hours. A numbness introduced into her body relieved her pain and enabled her to sleep more easily. Through hypnotic suggestion, she was helped to enjoy her food without her usual upset stomach. Hypnosis was so successful that her regular medication was cut back, and her relationships with her family improved considerably.

"Six weeks after her first trance, while laughing and talking to her daughter, she suddenly lapsed into a coma and died two days later without recovering. But those six weeks had been decidedly happy and pain-free for her."[14]

In terminal situations like the one that confronted Louise, hypnosis does not replace pain medication. Instead, it's used as a companion treatment which can frequently result in a greatly reduced need for drugs.

A second method of hypnosis is where the individual puts himself into a trance without a therapist's help. The self-hypnosis technique involves considerably more practice than hypnosis under the guidance of a specialist, but it is still possible for most of us.

One of the most interesting uses of self-hypnosis with cancer involved John Bennett of the Harvard Business School. Bennett was suffering from depression, nausea, and an earache from radiation therapy for a tumor at the back of his tongue. To relieve his distress, he began to use self-hypnosis which a friend had taught him.

"I had never used it before to any real purpose, but I started to do so while we were in Bermuda," he recalled. "It became a valuable tool. . . . Self-hypnotism makes one peculiarly receptive to one's own suggestion. . . . In almost daily sessions, I told myself that I would have peace of mind, strength, and joy."[15]

His specific technique involved devoting four or five minutes to self-hypnotism each day in his office or home. "I sat in some spot where I was free from interruption," he explained. "I stared fixedly at a spot a little above the horizon and counted slowly to three, timing each number to a full, deep breath. As I counted, my eyes closed and I was in hypnosis. I remained in full possession of my faculties, although they were focused inward. Then I repeated my suggestions for change. If I felt like doing so and had the time, I remained in hypnosis, relaxed and resting for a few more minutes. Or I roused myself as soon as I had repeated my suggestions by counting down from three to one. Somewhere in the count, my eyes opened and the hypnosis ended. After I had thoroughly mastered these simple techniques, I sometimes used a five-minute subway ride for self-hypnotism to repeat to myself my determination to have peace of mind, strength, and joy—and to be cured."

These techniques helped Bennett ward off his nausea, depression, and ear pain, and they could help you if you find yourself facing a serious or even deadly challenge to your health.

Hallucinogenic drugs and hypnosis may be necessary to elevate your mood and banish emotional anguish because of a lack of support and encouragement from other human beings. Even if your family members are always available and deeply concerned about your condition, they may not be able to provide the help you need to overcome anxiety and depression during the final stage of your life. I frequently have seen loved ones who hover around a terminally ill patient and lack the knowledge or will to enter into a meaningful discussion about his illness or his feelings. A quick, "My, how well you look!" is of little comfort.

A large number of people have been trained to fill this gap by working with the mental anguish of dying patients. These specialists include not only psychiatrists and psychologists, but also social workers, nurses, physicians, and clergy. Here are a few things a trained therapist can do to help when you're dying:

- Help you manage difficult feelings that you may be experiencing, such as fear, anger, and sadness.
- Act as an effective link between your family and the medical staff during those times when communication becomes difficult.
- Give you the assurance that you will have the presence of an understanding person with you until the end.
- Help you understand your feelings of guilt and unfulfillment and help you to complete emotionally unfinished business.

A sensitive, concerned family member who takes the time to learn how to help his dying loved one can be as helpful as a professional therapist. But if you can't find any friend or relative who can step into this role, seek out a professional. If he does his job, he'll help you cope better as the end of your life approaches.

In addition to the health professionals, various lay organizations counsel the dying. One of the most established is Orville Kelly's "Making Today Count." Kelly, who himself suffers from cancer, set up a series of support groups all around the country where people who share a similar plight can offer support to one another. Another lay group is "Shanti" in San Francisco. There, under the leadership of psychologist Dr. Charles Garfield, lay persons are trained in how to do effective intervention with the dying. Another lay group, but one which charges a fee, is "Threshold," founded by two businessmen in Southern California. There are others in addition to these mentioned. As in any lay organization, it is important for zeal to be tempered with knowledge and experience. One should make inquiries about what services are offered and who is doing the serving.

The purpose of LSD therapy, hypnosis, psychotherapy, and counseling during your last days is to free you from debilitating emotions, including a preoccupation with mental suffering and a lack of meaning that often accompany the dying process. Perhaps all you'll need to raise yourself from depression or to temper anxiety is a deep faith or a sensitive spouse or friend. If these resources are not enough, don't hesitate to explore the other means for keeping your spirits up as you approach the end of life. By reducing psychological stress during those final days, you may make the end of your life a time of poise, growth, and fulfillment.

1. Ted Rosenthal, *How Could I Not Be Among You?* (New York: Braziller, 1973), 52.
2. A. A. Kurland, et al., "Psychedelic Drug Assisted Psychotheraphy in Patients with Terminal Cancer," in I. K. Goldberg et al., *Psychopharmacologic Agents for the Terminally Ill and Bereaved* (New York: Foundation of Thanatology, Columbia U. Press, 1973), 87.
3. Eric C. Kast and V. J. Collins, "A Study of Lysergic Acid Diethylamide as an Analgesic Agent," *Anesthesia and Analgesia: Current Research* (1964), 291.
4. Kurland, op. cit., 89.
5. W. Richards, et al., "LSD-Assisted Psychotherapy and the Human Encounter with Death," *J. Transpersonal Psychology,* 4(1972), 121-150.
6. Ibid., 135.
7. Ibid., 137.
8. Ibid., 138.
9. Kurland, 99.
10. Ibid., 100.
11. Richards, op. cit., 146.
12. John Hinton, *Dying* (Baltimore: Penguin Books, 1967), 120.
13. Elisabeth Kubler-Ross, "On the Use of Psychopharmacologic Agents for the Dying Patient and the Bereaved," in I. K. Goldberg, et al., *Psychopharmacologic Agents for the Terminally Ill and Bereaved* (New York: Columbia U. Press, 1973), 6.
14. Milton H. Erickson, "Hypnosis in Painful Terminal Illness," *Amer. J. Clin. Hypnosis,* (1959).
15. John B. Bennett and Stanley E. Sagov, "An Experience of Cancer," *Harper's* (November, 1973), 94-102.

III

Freedom
From
Futility

Chapter Seven

FREE TO
RECYCLE YOURSELF

What will happen to your body after you die? For centuries philosophers and theologians have argued over what happens to man's spirit and his personality after death. There's less controversy about the fate of the physical body. As the Burial of the Dead ceremony in the *Book of Common Prayer* puts it, "Earth to earth, ashes to ashes, dust to dust. . . ."

Ashes make a mess as they accumulate in your fireplace, and dust is a constant hassle in keeping a house clean. Seems like a waste of good parts, doesn't it? Isn't there anything you can do with your marvelous body after you're finished with it, besides allowing it to disintegrate and litter the landscape?

Yes, you can recycle yourself, or at least part of yourself. In the ecology of death, you have several constructive choices about what to do with your body after you die. One of the most helpful and meaningful things you can do during your life is to arrange to donate your body organs for transplantation to people who will die sooner without them. Or you can give your body to medical research and help scientists take another step toward conquering a dread disease. Or finally, you can donate your physical remains for anatomical study, so that some medical student will be better prepared when he begins to treat his patients.

Do you personally know of anyone who has donated or received a body organ? If so, comment below.

The person is _____
His/her relationship to me is _____
The organ(s) donated was (were) _____
The attitude of the recipient or donor (if known) was _____

The chances are that you left the spaces blank because you don't know anyone who has received or donated an organ. Very few people are involved in the transplantation experience, but not because there isn't a great need. I worked with one young woman named Margaret who would have died five years ago if she hadn't received a kidney transplant.

Two of her brothers became sick and died of a kidney disorder before she had entered high school. Even though she knew her family was predisposed to kidney disease, Margaret had been a vibrant, fun-loving girl. She always felt quite safe from the disease itself because she thought this was something that only afflicted the male side of her family.

After high school graduation she married her high school sweetheart. Before the marriage, they decided not to have children because of the possibility of having children who might develop kidney disease. "That's okay with me," her husband said. "We can always adopt."

They had been married about a year when they adopted a little girl. Six months after the adoption, Margaret began to pass blood and suffered a burning sensation during urination.

Several physicians examined her and finally concluded that she, like her brothers, had very little chance of survival. In fact, they gave her only about five years to live. The impact of such news on this recent bride and new mother was devastating. She felt that she had everything to live for, and now her life was going to be cut short.

As her condition grew worse, she had to start using a dialysis machine—an artificial kidney. That involved going to the hospital twice a week for about ten hours each time to have her blood entirely cleansed by the machine.

Because of Margaret's medical condition and prognosis, the adoption agency was concerned about letting the adoption become final. Finally they decided to let her keep the baby, primarily because Margaret's doctors told her that she might be able to undergo a successful kidney transplant. Because no one in her immediate family had a healthy kidney, they had to put their hopes on a cadaver donor—a patient who had agreed before death to give his kidneys to someone like Margaret.

Margaret had to wait nearly two years before a suitable cadaver donor became available, and during that time her mood worsened. "Get away from me!" she shouted at her parents and even her husband. "I just want to be left alone."

Although she knew she was hurting those who loved her most,

she couldn't help herself. She especially hated being hooked up to the dialysis machine at regular intervals, because up to that point her life had been quite independent. She had been told that she had only a short time to live if she failed to get a new kidney. Unable to accept that prognosis, she became even more depressed.

Finally her doctors were able to find a suitable donor, and Margaret underwent a transplantation operation. The transformation in her personality and her outlook on life were close to miraculous. Her body accepted the new organ, and she experienced a sense of total freedom because she was no longer dependent on dialysis. She was given a new start in life, an indefinite postponement of certain death, because someone like you or me decided not to discard his body when he was finished with it.

Even after hearing about the obvious benefits of organ donation to Margaret, many people are still resistant to the idea. If you are also, try getting in touch with the source of your reluctance by looking at the resistances listed below. Check off the ones which apply to you.

_____ I'm afraid I might not be dead when they remove an organ.

_____ I'm chicken about doing unusual things.

_____ Organ donation is a fad.

_____ It's a sick, perverted idea.

_____ They wouldn't use my parts anyway.

_____ My kind don't do things like that.

_____ If I do anything with my body, I'll freeze it for possible later revival.

_____ I'm embarrassed and uncomfortable about having my dead body cut up or examined by doctors or medical students.

_____ I want to be buried intact.

_____ Removal of any organs might spoil my looks.

_____ It's too much trouble to arrange for organ donation before I die.

_____ I really don't care about medical research or helping people who need transplants.

_____ God wouldn't approve.

_____ I need all my parts for the afterlife.

———— It might hurt, since I don't know what death is like.
———— My relatives will donate my body organs if somebody
needs them.

Now that you have pinpointed some of your resistances, look at
some of them in more detail.

Fear.   Some people worry about whether physicians are com-
petent or concerned enough to ascertain when death actually
occurs. There has been a great deal of speculation lately, especially
in the popular press, that doctors may not always wait until a
patient is dead before they take an organ for a transplant
operation.

In one widely publicized case, Dr. Norman Shumway, the noted
Stanford University heart surgeon, removed the heart from a
murder victim and transplanted it to one of his patients. The
alleged murderer, Andrew D. Lyons, fatally shot the victim in the
head, according to the indictment. The victim was pronounced
"neurologically dead" by doctors independent of Shumway as a
result of an unconscious state and a lack of brain activity recorded
on an electroencephalogram (EEG).

But Lyons' defense lawyer challenged the conclusion that the
victim was actually dead. He argued that the heart was still beating
when it was removed for transplantation and that the surgeon, not
his client, had actually caused the death.

The trial judge rejected the defense argument, but another California judge ruled in a similar case that the removal of a heart,
which had been kept beating by mechanical devices, obscured the
cause of death. This second judge dismissed a homicide charge
against the defendant.

As these and other courts try to sort out a legal definition of
death, it's natural that a potential donor might be concerned. Is
there a chance you might not be dead before your organs are
removed? As a practical matter, you have nothing to worry about.
The courts are in flux now, trying to formulate an updated definition of death that will apply to every case. You, on the other
hand, will be treated as an individual by a personal physician who
will use several tests to determine your condition.

Attending physicians usually rely on traditional indications of death, such as the cessation of spontaneous muscular movements like respiration and heartbeat. If the patient is in a deep coma and on an artificial respirator, the usual way to determine death is to be certain that there is no spontaneous breathing for several minutes after the respirator is turned off.

The "brain death" test for death—also known as the "Harvard criteria," after a standard formulated by a Harvard University committee in 1968—has gained popularity and also fostered many misconceptions in recent years. This test requires a flat EEG for approximately forty-eight hours and *also* a physician's judgment of a lack of the traditional vital life signs, such as spontaneous respiration and heartbeat. Contrary to some current notions, the brain test is *not* used as an alternative to the traditional methods of death determination.[1] One of the main advantages of the Harvard criteria is that doctors can pronounce a patient dead and still keep his circulatory system going artificially so that his organs can be preserved for transplantation.

Regardless of what test is used, you don't have to worry that some doctor will decide you don't have a chance to live and kill you a little early to give an organ recipient a better chance of surviving. To insure there will be no conflict of interest between your attending physician and the transplantation team, there is a general requirement that the two responsibilities must be kept separate. In other words, the doctor who determines your death must be independent of the one who removes your organs.

So don't be concerned about whether you'll really be dead when they remove your organs. If you trust your doctor to prescribe medicine, deliver your baby, or take out your appendix, then trust him to be especially conscientious in deciding when the end of your life has arrived.

Ignorance.   If you said you think organ donation is sick or a fad, you're probably suffering from a lack of knowledge. As we explore some of the hard facts about transplants, we hope these objections will disappear.

Many people have picked up bits and pieces of information about a process called "cryonics," or freezing and storing the body in a vault in the hope that it can be revived later when medical technology has become more advanced. Perhaps such fantasies as the Woody Allen movie *Sleeper* have tantalized you with the idea that freezing may be a reasonable alternative to organ donation.

Most experts offer no hope that the bodies treated in this way will ever come back to life. Also, the equipment is bulky and requires regular changes of liquid nitrogen to keep the body temperature at a low level. The procedure costs thousands of dollars. Even if by some remote chance you could be revived, there's no guarantee that those who join a cryonics society or some similar group will be near enough to the freezing machinery at death to make the process worthwhile. In an accidental death, for example, the delay in transporting the deceased to a hospital or cryonics institute damages most brain cells beyond repair. And the freezing process itself damages tissues in ways that are probably too extensive to be corrected.

If you checked this response, perhaps you failed to consider the high expense of cryonics or the extremely remote chance that it will work. Freezing your body is probably just a waste of good tissues that could be donated at death to help extend another person's life.

Vanity. If you're worried that your donated body may be disfigured or treated disrespectfully, you're caught up in an emotional issue that can be very hard to resolve rationally. But remember, there are different types of body donation. The groups that support organ transplants stress the lack of disfigurement and the close working relationship transplant teams have with funeral directors.[2]

The most distasteful thing that might happen if you donate your body for anatomical study to a medical school is that some student might give your body a humorous name. But keep this in mind: he's just trying to lower his own PDA because he's being confronted directly with death. And because you chose to let him learn something from your body, he'll be in a better position to treat other human beings.

Laziness and indifference. These are probably the most common reasons for failing to donate organs after death. Even if you think it's a good thing to donate, you may believe it's too much trouble. In fact, it only takes a letter or a phone call to your local organ donation center and the filling out of a donor's card.

Religious considerations. Members of some religious groups have resisted the alteration or mutilation of the body after death. The Jewish tradition, for example, involves a great reverence for the body as God's creation. For this reason, Orthodox and Conservative Jews oppose total destruction through cremation. They believe God intended for the body to be kept in one piece at burial. Orthodox Jews have also resisted autopsies except to gain information that will save a neighbor's life, and are against experimentation with the human body by dissection. When it comes to transplantation to help a needy person, however, nearly all Jewish groups seem receptive.

Christian folklore has occasionally given rise to the idea that the believer's body should be kept intact for the eventual resurrection of the dead at Christ's Second Coming. But the traditional Christian position, as stated by the Apostle Paul in I Corinthians, 15, is quite different: "If there is a physical body, there is also a spiritual body. . . . Just as we have borne the image of the man of dust, we shall also bear the image of the man in heaven. I tell you this, brethren: flesh and blood cannot inherit the kingdom of God, nor does the perishable inherit the imperishable."

Representatives of all faiths have carefully considered the question of transplantation. Rather than go into an extensive theological discussion, let me point out what a committee at the National Heart Institute reported in 1969 when they took a look at the wide-ranging implications of cardiac transplant: "Except for the unresolved problem of a generally acceptable medical definition of death, transplantation does not seem to raise issues incongruent with Protestant, Jewish, or Catholic beliefs."[3]

Passing the buck. Don't count on leaving the decision up to your relatives. I've been around too many patients and their families to be willing to rely on any rational, unemotional decisions by the bereaved. The sense of loss may be so great that relatives think they can hold on a little longer, squeeze a little life out of the lifeless body that lies before them. Physicians are often unwilling to intrude on the family's sorrow to pose the donation question. And the longer they wait to make a decision, the less chance there is that your organs will be sufficiently viable for transplantation. If the donation decision is to be made, it should be made coolly and logically, well before you take your last breath.

Each year the demand for organs for transplantation and medical research far outstrips the number of donors. It's quite common for potential recipients to wait months or even years for a suitable donation. Many organs are needed for transplantation and research, but the eight major ones are the kidneys, eyes, inner ears, heart, skin, bones, pituitary glands, and liver. To understand how great the need is, take a closer look at each.

Kidneys.   By the end of 1975, more than 14,000 people in the United States had received kidney transplants.[4] Unfortunately, a large number of people—8,000—have died annually in the past because they couldn't get a transplant or obtain the regular use of a kidney machine.[5]

A federal law which went into effect on July 1, 1973, now requires the government, under Medicare, to provide dialysis treatment through kidney machines for patients with chronic renal diseases. The legislation applies to all people insured through Social Security—or approximately ninety percent of all American workers and their families, according to the National Kidney Foundation.

Although there have been many administrative problems in implementing the law, the prospects for survival by dialysis are much brighter now than in the past. During 1972, for example, only 800 people could be put on kidney machines, primarily because most patients couldn't afford the high costs. The usual expense at hospitals runs from $20,000 to $35,000 a year. If dialysis is done at home, the initial costs to set up the equipment run between $12,000 and $18,000, and subsequent annual costs are $5,000 to $10,000.

The new federal legislation also covers the cost of kidney transplantation, which is preferable to dialysis because it enables patients to live normal lives, free from dependence on a machine. But transplantation poses a special set of problems. The main difficulty is that there aren't enough organ donations to go around. In addition, there are many complex biological and chemical hurdles to clear so that the body won't reject a transplanted kidney. Although much progress has been made in finding tissues that will match, the chances of finding a suitable match in body chemistry between unrelated people is about one in a thousand.

Because there aren't enough post-mortem donors, you may ask why more living donors, closely related to the sick people, don't give their kidneys to their loved ones.

True, when the transplanted kidney comes from a living brother or sister, the chances for long-term survival are about ninety percent. And organ donations from parents have a high success rate, too. But because living related donors are hard to obtain, unrelated cadaver donors will have to remain the most common source for transplants. Some relatives simply refuse to submit to an operation and give up one of their organs. Others, because of their close relationship with the recipient, experience insurmountable psychological reactions to the idea of a transplant operation.

Consider Susan, a fifteen-year-old girl whose problem was diagnosed as a terminal kidney condition. Her mother decided to become a donor, but Susan was unhappy at the prospect of receiving her mother's organ. "It's going to hurt her!" she cried. "I don't want to be the one to hurt my mother."

After the transplant, serious problems developed which may have been related to these guilt feelings. Susan constantly ran a fever and attempted suicide on two occasions. Finally the kidney failed and had to be removed. She was put on dialysis. The girl blamed herself for her body's rejection of the kidney, and her feelings were reinforced when her mother began to withdraw from her both physically and emotionally.

"I don't have the money to keep visiting the girl in the hospital," the mother protested. "We live too far away. Besides, I've been neglecting my other kids during Susan's illness, and I've got to give them more of my time."

After a few weeks, a cadaver kidney became available, and another transplant operation was performed. Even though she experienced difficulty with the new organ, Susan seemed more able to overcome her fears. She knew her parents had separated, and her mother continued to avoid her, but she adjusted to hospital life more easily than before.

With the help of the hospital staff, the mother began to see her daughter more often. Susan's body finally rejected the second kidney. A third transplant attempt failed, but the girl's outlook on life and her relationship with her mother had improved immeasurably. She remained in an optimistic mood and was more cheerful than before her transplants, even though she knew her chances of survival were decreasing each day.

Finally, in her seventh month of hospitalization, Susan asked for her mother to come to the hospital immediately. A few minutes after her mother arrived, she grabbed a nurse's hand and said, "Something is happening." Then she died.

It's unfortunate that Susan couldn't have been one of the longer-lived transplantation success stories. But even for the brief time that she survived the cadaver transplant, her outlook improved because she didn't confront the psychological entanglements that arose with her mother's kidney. The cadaver kidney encouraged Susan to become more independent of her mother and also gave her several extra months to iron out family difficulties and prepare herself for a more meaningful death.

Given the rejection rate and the difficulty of matching up donors and recipients, there should be about eight million kidney donors *every year* to insure all those with renal diseases a chance at a successful transplant. It's been estimated that only about 200,000 people have arranged to donate any part of their bodies to science, much less their kidneys. The number of post-mortem kidney donors, in other words, is woefully inadequate to the need.

Eyes. In eye medicine, about 4,000 corneal transplants are performed each year,[6] and eighty to ninety percent are successful on the first try. Approximately 30,000 men and women who are partially or totally blind could regain most of their sight through this operation.

In recent years, surgery using the white part of the eye, the sclera, and also the spongy interior tissue, the vitreous humor, has been tried on a smaller scale. Even diseased eyes are needed for study of eye disorders and anatomy. Eye parts, of course, can't be taken from living donors.

Eyes are removed from donors about six to eight hours after death, and pieces of moist cotton about the size of the eye are placed in the sockets. A few small stitches are then taken to close the eyelids. When a person is lying in his casket, it's impossible to tell if he had made a donation.

According to Maryellen McEvoy, Executive Director of the New England Eye Bank,[7] there are approximately two hundred people on the waiting list for transplants at the Massachusetts Eye and Ear Infirmary at any one time. Because of the great demand, prospective recipients may have to wait from three months to a year for a chance at improved sight.

Ears.   The temporal bones or inner ears are what we're talking about here. The donor's outer ears remain undisturbed when this part is removed, so there's no disfigurement for funeral purposes. Dr. Rodney Perkins of Project Hear in Palo Alto, California, established an eardrum and ossicle (earbone) bank in 1969, and he's had some success in relieving deafness by transplanting these parts.[8] A large number of damaged or impaired inner ears are also needed for research by the Temporal Bone Bank in Maryland.[9]

Heart.   In the late 1960s heart surgeons became the glamor boys in the transplant field because of the apparent miracles they were able to perform. But despite all the publicity, they have done barely 200 heart transplants, as compared to the approximately 14,000 kidney transplant operations.

The spotlight on men like South Africa's Dr. Christiaan Barnard and Texas' Dr. Michael DeBakey lasted only briefly. Heart transplantation operations fell off sharply after 1969 because the results of the operations failed to live up to expectations. Dr. Norman Shumway of Stanford University has done most of the operations since 1970.[10]

Although there is some indication that we may be on the verge of a resurgence of heart transplants, the number will probably remain comparatively small because of the difficulty of the operation. But I believe heart donation is justified if only because heart recipients have survived up to six years after the transplant.

Skin and bones. Skin and bone tissue are collected immediately after the donor's death by the United States Naval Tissue Bank in Bethesda, Maryland. The Naval Medical Research Institute, which has pioneered in the development of storage methods for human tissue, gets many donations from dead Navy personnel and their families.

The skin is used as a dressing in cases of severe, extensive burns and is more effective than ordinary cloth bandages. The transferred tissue does not itself grow, but conserves body fluids and encourages faster growth of new skin.

Transplanted bones can also help replace destroyed bones. A cadaver donor's bones can be combined with marrow from the patient's own body and then transferred to the location of the destroyed bone. The patient's own bone tissue then begins to copy the transplanted bone and slowly absorbs it.

One of the most startling success stories in bone transplantation involved a marine whose lower jaw was shattered by a gunshot in Vietnam.[11] The loss of his mandible, or jawbone, made it impossible for him to speak, and he could not breathe without a tracheotomy tube. His tongue protruded from his mouth, and he drooled constantly.

Another man's mandible, which had been frozen at the donor's death and deposited in a tissue bank at the Naval Medical Research Institute in Bethesda, Maryland, was combined with bone marrow from the marine's own hip. This new jawbone was then transplanted to the young man's face, and teeth and skin grafts were eventually implanted in the new bone structure. Two years after his original injury, the marine was able to talk and eat normally, and his appearance improved dramatically.

Using similar techniques, scientists are also having some success in combating aplastic anemia, a blood disease, with marrow transplants and in transferring frozen bone chips to living bodies.

Pituitary glands. This pea-sized organ of growth is located underneath the brain in the skull. About 5,000 young children suffer from hypopituitarism, a deficiency in their own growth glands which causes them to remain dwarfs.[12] Each of these children needs the extracts from 120 adult glands every year until he reaches his full adult size. In other words, to meet the need completely, about seventy-five percent of all those who die in this country every year—or nearly a million people—would have to donate their glands to the National Pituitary Agency.

Surgeons remove the pituitary by making an incision in the base of the skull, which is not disfiguring.

Liver. There's still little hope for the heavy drinker whose drinking damages his liver, but a few people have been able to prolong their lives through the very complex liver transplant operation. One recipient lived nearly five years after the procedure. Most headway has been made with those suffering from Wilson's disease, a rare genetic malady involving defective control of copper in the body.[13]

Altogether, there are about twenty-five different types of organs and tissues that have been used in transplantation operations. The lungs, pancreas, spleen, and many others have been transferred from cadaver donors to living recipients, but the success rate with most of them has been far more disappointing than with the eight discussed.

It's likely that your Personal Death Awareness is rather high now, maybe even uncomfortably so. The discussion of organ donation may seem threatening, but you are probably also experiencing some ambivalence because the idea of helping another person live longer or aiding scientific research appeals to you. Give in to the positive side of your ambivalence and consider how to go about donating one or more of your organs.

Most people donate their body parts for transplantation or their entire bodies for research by using the Uniform Donor Card. This card has been made a binding legal document in all fifty states by laws which are based on the Uniform Anatomical Gift Act.

This law cuts through bureaucratic red tape and gives the dead person's decision to donate priority over the claims of surviving relatives. If you're eighteen years old (twenty-one in some states) and sane, you can call or write to the American Medical Association, the National Kidney Foundation, or a number of other health organizations for the wallet-sized donor card. When you receive the card, all you have to do is fill it out, have it signed by two witnesses, and carry it in your wallet.

It's legally effective no matter where you die in the United States.

With the exception of cornea donors, transplant centers prefer to have the organs of people who are under sixty years of age. Also, your donated organs should be free of disease. If you want to give your body for anatomical study, only your eyes may be removed for transplantation.

"But what if I change my mind?" you may protest. "What if I decide next month I don't want to donate my body?"

If you change your mind, there's no problem. All you have to do is tear up your donor card, and you're right back where you started. Some organizations, like the National Kidney Foundation, keep track of their card holders by having them send in a name and address card that detaches from the donor card. But these file cards have no legal effect after you destroy your donor card. There's no registration requirement and it's not necessary for you to include anything about organ donation in your will.

The donor card also allows you to place a limit on which organs you give. If you want to donate only your eyes or pituitary gland, for example, you can specify these restrictions on your card.

But do be aware of a few popular misconceptions: Signing the donor card does *not* free your survivors from paying your funeral expenses. Nor does anyone get paid anything for the organs you donate.

Before signing a donor card, you should talk the issue over with your family. It's much easier to get in touch with your true feelings and theirs in a dispassionate setting, rather than during a deathbed scene. Your doctor, lawyer, and clergyman should also be informed of your decision so that when you're not around to explain your wishes, things can move along more smoothly.

If you decide to become a donor, the chances of your body being put to constructive use are quite good, provided certain conditions are met. Major organs like the kidney must be taken almost immediately after death, so it's usually important that you be in or near a hospital when you die. Removal of your eyes, on the other hand, can be done up to eight hours after death. Even if your organs are found unsuitable for transplantation, they can often be used for research purposes.

Scientific advances in organ storage and transplantation techniques have made it possible for hospitals that were once considered too remote, to contribute organs to transplant centers. Kidneys, for example, can now be removed and preserved up to seventy hours before the transplantation is performed.

There's also a nationwide computer network to match up the most compatible kidney donors with potential recipients. Usually, however, the need is so great at most locations that there is rarely any effort made to fly a kidney to distant locations.

Here is a copy of the Uniform Donor Card. Try filling it out.

UNIFORM DONOR CARD

OF _____
(Print or type name of donor)

In the hope that I may help others, I hereby make this anatomical gift, if medically acceptable, to take effect upon my death. The words and marks below indicate my desires.

I give: (a)_____any needed organs or parts
          (b)_____only the following organs or parts

_____
(Specify the organ(s) or part(s))

for the purposes of transplantation, therapy, medical research or education;

          (c)_____my body for anatomical study if needed.

Limitations or
special wishes, if any: _____

[Other Side of Card]

Signed by the donor and the following two witnesses in the presence of each other:

Signature of Donor	Date of Birth of Donor
Date Signed	City and State
Witness	Witness

This is a legal document under the Uniform Anatomical Gift Act or similar laws.

If you find that you do want to donate and you have little resistance to the idea, let me encourage you to obtain a donor card today from one of these addresses. Each group sends the same card. Don't put it off, or you may lose the chance to have your wishes fulfilled.

General Information
American Medical Association, 535 N. Dearborn St., Chicago, Ill. 60610.
National Transplant Information Center, 135 Flower Hill Road, Huntington, N. Y. 11743.

Kidneys
National Kidney Foundation, Inc., 116 East 27th St., New York, N. Y. 10016.
National Association of Patients on Hemodialysis and Transplantation, P. O. Box 60, Brooklyn, N. Y. 11203.

Eyes
The Eye Bank Association of America, 3195 Maplewood Ave., Winston-Salem, N. C. 27013
The Eye Bank for Sight Restoration, Inc., 210 East 64th St., New York, N. Y. 10021.

Pituitary Glands
National Pituitary Agency, Suite 503-7, 210 West Fayette St., Baltimore, Maryland 21201.

Inner ears
Project Hear, Rodney Perkins, M.D., 1801 Page Mill Road, Palo Alto, California 94304.

I'm very familiar with the resistances you may be experiencing in making this decision because I've had them myself. I had a donor card sitting on my desk for several months before finally filling it out. I found that *intellectually* I was in favor of the idea of donation. I had worked with many whose lives had been lengthened because of organ donation. But I still found myself hesitant *emotionally* to fill out one of the cards. My main problem was that I view my body as a very personal and private thing, and I wasn't sure I wanted anyone messing with it after I was dead. But finally I broke free from my reservations and filled out a donor card.

At this point, I'm willing to give my eyes and kidneys after I die. It gives me great satisfaction to know that by facing my death squarely, by making a decision now about the final disposition of my body, I may help free someone from a kidney machine or play a role in restoring his sight. The only inconvenience for me was to take a few moments to fill in a donor card. The benefits for the individual who will carry my kidney or cornea cannot be measured by time, however, but only by an improvement in the quality of life.

Perhaps at a later time I'll want to give additional organs, but this is where I stand at present. What about you? If you believe that donation is a good idea, do something about it now! You will reap the good feeling that you are doing something which will benefit others and also have the sense of satisfaction that a part of you will live on after you are gone.

1. "Refinements in Criteria for the Determination of Death: An Appraisal," *JAMA*, 221 (July 3, 1972), 48-53.
2. I. Ladimer, "The Challenge of Transplantation," *Public Affairs Pamphlet No. 451*, New York, 1970, 14.
3. R. T. Eastwood, et al., *Cardiac Replacement: Medical, Ethical, Psychological and Economic Implications*, A Report by the Ad Hoc Task Force on Cardiac Replacement, National Heart and Lung Institute, NIH, Washington, D.C., G.P.O., 1969, 38-39.
4. Personal Communication, National Kidney Foundation, Inc., 116 East 27th St., N.Y., N.Y. 10016.
5. "Dialysis of Kidney Patients," *National Kidney Foundation*, pamphlet.
6. Personal communication, The Eye Bank Association of America, 3195 Maplewood Ave., Winston-Salem, N.C. 27103.
7. Personal Communication with M. McEvoy, Executive Director, New England Eye Bank, Boston, Mass. 02114.
8. Rodney Perkins, Project Hear, Palo Alto, California.
9. "The Temporal Bone Banks Program for Ear Research," Deafness Research Foundation, New York, New York.
10. "World Total Heart Transplants," and "Survivors of Human Heart Transplantation," Organ Transplant Registry, June 1, 1973, Chicago, Illinois.
11. Cdr. H. O. de Fries, MC, USN; Capt. H. B. Marble, DC, USN; Cdr. K. W. Sell, MC, USN, "Reconstruction of the Mandible," *Archives of Otolaryngology*, 93 (April, 1971), 426-432.
12. "This Child is a Dwarf," National Pituitary Agency, Baltimore, Maryland.
13. "Liver Transplant Picture Brightens Slowly," *JAMA*, 223 (Feb. 5,1973), 603-605.

Chapter Eight

FREE TO
GIVE TO OTHERS

As he began his final year of study, a medical student from the South was looking forward to a successful career. Because he expected he would have plenty of money soon after graduation, he rarely thought about personal finances. But when his young wife became pregnant, he decided it might be wise to check into getting some life insurance.

He talked to a couple of insurance agents and learned that the premiums could be kept quite low while he was still in school. But he hesitated. "Why not wait until I graduate?" he asked one salesman. "I'll have plenty of money then."

"It's nearly a year until your graduation," the agent replied. "What will happen to your wife and unborn child if you die before then?"

"But I'm not going to die!" the student retorted, laughing. "I'm in good health."

Finally he decided to postpone buying a policy. Two months before he was scheduled to graduate, he was reaching up for some equipment in his hospital and pulled some shelving over on himself. He was crushed against the floor, and died instantly. His wife, still pregnant, was left with nothing but the memory of her husband and of the secure life they might have led. The young medical student's untimely death resulted in serious financial difficulties for his family.

"Ours is a business of death," Dallas insurance man Joe Miller says. "Nothing good can happen until the insured person dies. It's no fun to talk about death. It's so negative. I'd rather talk about things that are more positive."

But Miller and other insurance men, lawyers, and estate planners know that if they're going to help clients, they have to confront the threatening subject of death. Many of our important financial decisions, including life insurance and wills, depend on the fact that we're going to die. We postpone our estate planning—our decisions about what to do with our possessions after we die—because thinking about such things raises our Personal Death Awareness to an uncomfortable level. Rather than facing and conquering the uneasiness that may accompany a high PDA, we often prefer to project an indefinite life span for ourselves.

Take a close look at your family situation. Has a low PDA kept you from making important financial decisions? If you died today, what would happen to your survivors? Or consider the other side: if your spouse died, what would happen to *you*? Take an inventory and see which responses best describe the present state of your finances and financial attitudes:

1. With regard to wills:
   _____ I have a will.
   _____ I do not have a will.
   _____ My spouse has a will.
   _____ My spouse does not have a will.
2. I have $_____ insurance on my life.
3. If I died today, my insurance would provide my family with
   _____ the same standard of living.
   _____ a lower standard of living.
   _____ a higher standard of living.
4. I don't carry insurance because
   _____ relatives will take care of my family.
   _____ my wife/husband has a good job or job skills and wouldn't need insurance.
   _____ I haven't had time to buy a policy.
   _____ I believe all insurance men are just out to make a buck.
   _____ After I die, I don't care who gets what.

Because people who sell insurance, plan estates, and write wills often make a good living from their fees, it's easy to rationalize that they are just out to make money from the sale of unnecessary services. Such an attitude involves a misconception of the facts. One clear-cut example of the need for insurance is the case of an elderly widow I know whose husband, at the time he died, had accumulated about $15,000 in savings and investments. They had been accustomed to living on $15,000 a year, and there was no way that their small estate would allow her to live even at a subsistence level.

Just as she was about to sell her house, she heard from her

husband's company that she was the beneficiary of a large group insurance policy on his life. Remembering he had mentioned something about other policies, she looked through his personal papers and found that her total insurance benefits amounted to $85,000. With a total estate of about $100,000, she was in a position to maintain her former standard of living and had one less thing to worry about as she grieved her husband's death.

Situations like this suggest to me that estate planning, regardless of how much or how little you own, is essential. Life insurance seems to be the first and perhaps the most difficult hurdle for most people to cross. As insurance man Joe Miller put it, insurance is a "business of death," and most people would prefer to avoid the subject. For the past thirteen years, Miller has been on the insurance industry's élite Million Dollar Round Table, which requires its members to sell a minimum of $1 million in ordinary life insurance annually. He has had lengthy conversations with hundreds of people about putting their finances in order before they die. His work has made him an expert in the way that fear and denial of death can foreclose choices and reduce our freedom over the material things we own.

Miller has found two general categories of insurance prospects. "The first group are lacking in character," he explained. "They don't care about anything or anyone but themselves."

On one occasion, he visited a family in which the husband had a wife and two children, but no life insurance. As they were sitting around the couple's kitchen table, Miller said to the man, "Let me describe some of the financial needs your wife and kids may face after you die."

But before he could continue, the husband said, "I don't care what happens to my family after I die."

The insurance agent stopped talking. "I don't believe what you said," he replied.

"I don't have any obligations after I'm gone," the man declared.

"Do you really mean that?" Miller asked.

"I do."

Then Miller looked at the man and said, "I'm sorry. I guess we have nothing to talk about," and he left without another word.

Although Miller finds such people "frightening," he is happy that they at least seem to be in a minority. A more prevalent attitude is reflected in a second group who react to the life insurance issue by trying to ignore it.

"These people know that they have a problem, but they don't want to face it," Joe Miller says. "Some things, like death, are just too painful to think about. But somebody's going to have to think about them at some point. Somebody will eventually pay. A husband may pay a small amount each month while he's alive; or if he's failed to buy insurance, the wife and children will have to pay more than the premiums for food and rent after he's dead."

Estate planning experts have devised a number of methods for overcoming people's resistance to confronting their own deaths. Investment counselor Shelley Ivey, who has been advising clients about the purchase of insurance, stocks, and bonds in New York City for the past nineteen years, says that a basic principle he follows in discussing insurance is to "never talk about drawn-out, painful kinds of dying. I always tell people to imagine what would happen to their families if they got hit by a truck. Somehow, that's easier for them to deal with because they don't think they'll ever be killed that way. But at least they start thinking about their estate problems."

This hit-by-a-truck conversational ploy enables his clients to plan for their families without raising their PDA too much. "They don't have to face the reality that death may overcome them slowly, perhaps making them invalids before they finally pass on," Ivey explained.

One of the most subtle indirect methods Miller used was to tell upwardly mobile young prospects that they should consider the estate taxes they would probably have to pay. Most of these young people didn't have large estates as he talked to them, but they *expected* to—and liked to think about their future success. "When you talk about such matters, death is deferred in the mind of the listener because he's thinking about his success period," Miller explained. "Sure, he's going to die, but before he dies, he's going to do very well and make a lot of money. The negative of death becomes surrounded by a huge positive—success during life."

Miller is now less inclined to sidestep the issue of death, primarily because his religion has made him more comfortable with his mortality. His higher level of Personal Death Awareness has given him more freedom to consider the implications of death for himself, as well as for his clients. He still dislikes talking about death, but he can handle it in a more straightforward way when the occasion arises.

Just recently, he said to a potential client, "Look, you need more insurance. You've procrastinated, and I want you to buy some this week. If you die without it, I'm not going to be able to face your wife. And you don't have to buy it from me, either."

Miller has found that the greatest believers in life insurance are "people who have faced the abyss. Some people have had warnings or premonitions of death, such as a heart attack or some other physical problem. But if you wait for one of these warnings, you probably won't be able to qualify physically for an insurance policy."

The time to act is now, while you're still healthy—and insurable. In deciding on your life insurance program, you should sit down and evaluate what the financial impact would be if you or your spouse dies. What would it cost to replace the breadwinner's salary? If the spouse in charge of domestic chores or the children should die, would the survivor have to hire a maid or a nurse for the children?

Here are some additional questions that Shelley Ivey, Joe Miller, and other financial counselors suggest you consider in determining how much insurance to buy:

1. Will relatives on either side of the family automatically step in and help out?
2. Does the housewife have an occupational skill that would help her get a job?
3. How much insurance would it take to give each spouse peace of mind *now* about the family's financial situation in case the other dies?
4. How much could you afford for insurance premiums without depriving your family of things you consider necessary for your present happiness and well-being?

In deciding on the amount of insurance you need, don't let your prejudices against brash insurance salesmen you may know prevent you from facing the financial implications of your death. Contact a couple of insurance agents, compare the programs they offer, and take some positive action to provide for your family's needs.

Although insurance is an important choice, drafting of a will may be even more significant. At the outset, let me stress that the laws of each state on wills are quite different, so any generalizations we make here will have limited application. You'll have to check with your own lawyer to find the exact legal requirements where you live. If you don't have a lawyer, you can get one through your state or local bar association or legal aid society.

Many married couples assume that the husband should have a will, but that the wife doesn't need one because it's likely she will outlive her spouse and have time to make her own will. David Fuller, a New York attorney, points out that this attitude ignores the possibility that the husband and wife may die in the same disaster, within minutes or a few hours of each other.

"If the husband and wife die in the same accident and the wife survives slightly longer than the husband, she may not have time to make out a will," Fuller explains. "In that situation, the family's property will pass from the husband to the wife by will, but by operation of law it will then pass from the wife to her heirs without a will."

"What's wrong with that?" you may ask. In New York and in many other states, Fuller says, there are at least two significant problems, depending on whether the couple has children. If the couple is childless and the entire estate passes through the wife, her family will receive all the couple's money and property. *Nothing* will go to the husband's family if he dies first.

If you live in New York and that's what you want, then perhaps you don't need a will. But most people would prefer to see that the benefits of their estate are spread more equally, or at least directed toward those family members who are most in need. To exercise this control over your estate, you need a will.

If the couple has children and the wife dies without a will shortly after her husband, the children in a state like New York will receive all the property. This result may be in accordance with your wishes, but there is one major difficulty. "If you have small children," Fuller says, "You should have a will to name the person you'd like to have take care of them and manage the property they will receive. Otherwise, you may be setting the stage for a custody fight between other relatives. A court may be forced to appoint a guardian whom you might not have selected if you had decided the issue before your death."

There are many other reasons for having a will. If the husband doesn't have a will and he dies first, in most states his property will be divided between his wife and children. The children *may* turn their shares over to their widowed mother. But then again, the widow may get less than her husband actually would have provided had he made a will.

A will does just what its name implies: the document is an expression of what you *will* or *choose* to happen after you die. If you don't make a will, you forfeit control over those choices.

Such was the case for an elderly woman, Harriet, who asked a young nurse, Sandy, to care for her in her old age. In payment, Harriet promised that after her death, the house in which the two of them lived would go to the nurse. The details of exactly how the house was to pass to her were never discussed, because both women found death too unpleasant a subject for discussion.

Sandy devoted many of her evenings for several years to the care of her elderly companion. She did much of the housework, read to Harriet after she became bedridden, and performed many other tasks which were more valuable than the room, board, and meager allowance she was paid.

After Harriet died, Sandy notified the dead woman's family about the house agreement. But Harriet's son, the family spokesman, replied, "There was no will. How do we know that's what you and my mother agreed to?"

Sandy was stunned. She had devoted nearly three years of her life to Harriet, and she expected something in return. A friend who knew Harriet's family said, "Don't worry, I'm sure they'll provide something for you." But Sandy waited month after month, and all she had to show for her patience was a number of inconclusive phone calls.

Finally, she decided to hire a lawyer. He confirmed that she had no right to the house because Harriet had failed to leave a will. The attorney did begin negotiations with the family and got a small sum in settlement to cover some of the extra effort and expenses Sandy had incurred in nursing Harriet. But Sandy should have made sure that the full repayment for her services was in black and white—in a will or perhaps in a joint ownership arrangement for the house. Unfortunately, she and Harriet always avoided the topic of death because of their apparently low level of Personal Death Awareness. The resulting failure to draft a will subverted the desires of Harriet to compensate her attentive young friend, and also put Sandy at a serious financial disadvantage.

Especially if you're married or have someone who depends on you financially, it's extremely important to increase your own death awareness and take a hard look at your family estate plan. Because of your concern for the welfare of your loved ones, you will want to set your own affairs in order. And from a purely selfish point of view, you should encourage your spouse to get some insurance and make a will so that *you* can avoid financial difficulties.

There's a feeling of well-being that accompanies a decision to be responsible for any important aspect of your life, including the management of your material possessions. Constructive planning and organization of your estate will contribute to an inner sense of security, freedom, and power. You can move through life knowing that financial matters will be taken care of if death catches you unawares.

Chapter Nine

FREE TO LIVE UNTIL DEATH

When you're young and healthy, it's hard to imagine what it's like to be old and feeble—to be bedridden or close to death, day after day, and month after month. Most of us enjoy a relatively pleasant existence which we assume will continue until we take our last breath.

Chances are, things won't always be so easy. As you reach a relatively advanced age, it's possible that the quality of your life will decline significantly. You may lose your ability to move about, to communicate effectively with others, to be physically comfortable and free of pain. A powerful account of how unpleasant it can be to be old and ill—and how hard it can be to communicate feelings to younger people, including trained physicians—was described by Dr. Nancy Caroline, a resident at the University Hospitals in Cleveland.[1]

Dr. Caroline was assigned to treat a seventy-eight-year-old patient named Mr. Kahn, who had been admitted to the hospital following abdominal pains and vomiting. X-rays showed he had a bowel obstruction that would probably require surgery. When the physician walked over to introduce herself to Mr. Kahn, she saw he was thin and frail, but had marvelously bright eyes. He was staring at a patient next to him, Mr. Kovanich, who had just undergone an operation for cancer of the colon. Kovanich was breathing laboriously, as he lay entwined in a tangle of drains and tubes.

When he saw the doctor, Kahn said, "I'm dying."

"Don't be silly," she replied. "You are in a university hospital, equipped with all the latest technology. Here you must get well."

"My time has come."

"Time is measured differently here," the young physician said.

"What do you understand about time?" Mr. Kahn retorted. "Wait until you have lived seventy-eight years. Wait until you are seventy-eight years old and tired and alone and have a pain in your belly."

116

After an examination, Dr. Caroline decided to pass a tube into his stomach to decompress the bowel for a few days before attempting surgery. "We have to pass a tube down into your stomach, Mr. Kahn," she said.

"Like that?" he gestured toward the tube protruding from Kovanich's nose.

"Something like that."

"Listen, doctor. I don't want to die with tubes sticking out all over me," he said. "I don't want that my children should remember their father that way. All my life I tried to be a mensch, you understand? All my life I tried to live so I could hold my head up. Rich I wasn't, but I managed. I put my sons through college. I wanted to be able to hold my head up, to have dignity, even though I didn't have much money and didn't speak good English.

"Now, I'm dying. Okay. I'm not complaining. I'm old and tired and have seen enough of life, believe me. But still I want to be a man, not a vegetable that someone comes and waters every day." He looked over at Kovanich. "Not like him."

"We're trying to make you feel well again," the doctor answered.

He seemed suddenly tired of the conversation. "You don't understand," he said more to himself than to her.

Then they had to put another tube into Kahn—an intravenous to keep him from becoming dehydrated. He accepted it, but kept looking over at Kovanich.

Early the following morning, Kovanich had a heart attack. As the physicians worked over him, he was lying naked on his bed in a pool of excretions. For an hour they pounded his chest, squeezed air into his lungs, injected one medication after another, tried to thread a pacemaker down into his jugular vein. But Kovanich never recovered. Finally they removed his body from the room. Mr. Kahn had been watching the entire procedure.

Dr. Caroline was about to leave the room with the others. "Doctor, wait a minute," he said.

"What is it, Mr. Kahn?"

His eyes were frantic. "I want you should promise you'll never do that to me."

"Mr. Kahn, I know this has been very upsetting. . . "

"Promise!" he insisted, leaning forward in bed.

"All right, Mr. Kahn, I promise."

A few days later, Kahn suffered congestive heart failure. The house staff swung into action with morphine, oxygen, tourniquets, digitalis, diuretics. But he responded poorly and was having a lot of trouble breathing. Another physician suggested a tube to help him breathe. Kahn whispered to Dr. Caroline, "You promised. . . ."

"But this is different, Mr. Kahn," she replied. "This tube is just for a short while—maybe just a day. It's to help you breathe."

His face became expressionless, his eyes dull. Sometime late that night, Kahn woke up, reached over and switched off his ventilator. The nurses found him several hours later and called Dr. Caroline in to pronounce him dead. On the bedside table, she found a note, scrawled in Kahn's uneven hand: "Death is not the enemy, doctor. Inhumanity is."

The problem with improved medical technology is that even though you may have little or no chance of recovery, it's possible to keep you alive for long periods through extraordinary or "heroic" measures, with machines and tubes that keep your heart pumping and lungs breathing. Many times, from the patient's point of view, the quality of life may deteriorate so far that death is actually preferable. Mr. Kahn chose death over an inferior quality of life.

Although it may be desirable to die before the quality of life degenerates to an overwhelming burden, the issue is usually not completely clear-cut. Those who strenuously advocate the "right to die," for example, may overlook that terminating all a person's life support systems can actually result in considerable discomfort. The removal of intravenous tubes, drugs, and oxygen can cause a patient to suffer dehydration, fear of suffocation, and actual physical pain. No matter how much psychological preparation has preceded death, it can be nullified if the physician and the patient's family make the wrong decision about discontinuing extraordinary life support.

Even if you decide that "pulling the plug" won't cause pain or discomfort, you may still resist the elimination of these extraordinary measures. In your mind, rejecting medical treatment of any kind may smack of "mercy killing," euthanasia, or even suicide.

There are a variety of views on this issue, but in general, most religious groups seem to recognize a distinction between prolonging life when there's no hope, and cutting a life short when there may be hope. A statement adopted by the Council for Christian Social Action of the United Church of Christ declares that "nothing in Jewish or Christian tradition" requires a physician to impose his wishes about prolonging life on a patient if the patient is terminally ill and doesn't want the doctor's intervention.[2]

"People who are dying have as much freedom as other living persons to accept or refuse medical treatment where that treatment provides no cure for their ailment," the Council said. But the group made a distinction between this refusal to help the terminally ill and "suicide where the person makes the decision to die. Here, the illness or, depending on one's theology, God, has already made death imminent."[3]

In other words, when death becomes a question not of *if* but of *when*, many religious arguments against ending life seem to disappear. Many Roman Catholics, who have always strongly opposed any form of euthanasia or suicide, take a similar position. According to the Ethical and Religious Directives for Catholic Health Facilities, "Euthanasia in all forms is forbidden.... However, neither the physician nor the patient is obliged to the use of extraordinary means."

As an example of such extraordinary treatment, the directives say, "It is not euthanasia to give a dying person sedatives and analgesics for the alleviation of pain, when such a measure is judged necessary, even though they may deprive the patient of the use of reason *or shorten his life.*"[4]

Sister Annette Caron, a Catholic hospital administrator, acknowledges that death is an enemy that should be conquered. But she argues, "heroic measures to keep a patient alive by means of a resuscitator [and other such methods] are not required or advisable in certain circumstances. The extraordinary means to prolong the breathing processes are not, according to the medical and moral ethics of the Catholic church, required or encouraged."[5]

On your deathbed, you may be in a coma or be too weak to insist that your doctors take a specific course of action in treating you. The final decision about extraordinary measures will then be left up to your physicians and family. This was the issue posed in the recent, widely-publicized Karen Anne Quinlan case in Morristown, New Jersey. Miss Quinlan fell into a coma which lasted for many months, and her life was being sustained by a respirator. Her parents wanted to have the respirator removed so that she could die a natural death, but her doctors refused, and the case was thrown into the courts for a final decision.

If you should end up in an extended coma, is there any way your case might be resolved more smoothly, with less strain on your loved ones? Although there can be no absolute assurance that your wishes will be followed, there are certain steps you can take now, to influence the decisions your family and physicians may have to make.

1. **Your physician.** At a recent meeting, the American Medical Association officially went on record as opposed to "mercy killing." But the group also adopted a "death with dignity" resolution. In part, this statement declared that it's up to the patient or his immediate family to decide whether to use extraordinary means to prolong life. According to a recent Harris Poll, most American adults seem to agree with this opinion. The pollsters posed this proposition: "A patient with a terminal disease ought to be able to tell his doctor to let him die rather than extend his life when no cure is in sight." "Yes" was the response of sixty-two percent of those polled.

Most physicians try to follow the desires of the patient or immediate family, but it's important for you and your loved ones to take a close look at the attitudes of the doctor who will probably be handling your case. Dr. James J. Gill, S.J., a colleague of mine who is a physician at the Harvard Medical School, suggests a series of questions that you can ask your doctor:[6]

- Does he feel obliged to prolong life at all costs?
- Does he feel that *he* should make the decision about when life should end?
- Will he ever administer, either personally or through someone else, a drug in such quantity that it could prove fatal? Under what circumstances would he do so?

• Does he thoroughly subscribe to his hospital's official policy (if one has been formulated) pertaining to euthanasia in its various forms?

Gill concludes that you and your family members should never hesitate to learn how your doctor's personal sense of morality influences his medical practice. Determining the doctor's exact position on prolonging your life, Gill says, will probably "serve to promote an atmosphere of trust and confidence, mutual cooperation, and peace of soul for the patient, family and physician as well."

2. Your family. Even if you find a compatible physician, the final decision about the kind of care you'll receive will, in most cases, be in the hands of your family. If you've been close-mouthed on your preferences, your family may be confused or ambivalent about whether or when to allow you to be taken off extraordinary life-support systems. And if they decide to let you die, they may be plagued by guilt feelings afterward.

Professional counselors, such as chaplains, social workers, and psychologists, can help your family make this decision, but it will be much easier on them if you express your wishes ahead of time.

Paul exemplifies a man who gave his family some guidance. He began to think seriously about the issue of prolonging life when he visited a terminally-ill friend in a hospital. "If you are ever called upon to make such a decision, I don't want my life prolonged if you're sure I won't recover," he told his sons. "I'd rather not be kept alive indefinitely on a machine, like some vegetable."

Sometime later, Paul suffered a massive stroke which severely damaged his brain. His wife and sons had to decide how much treatment he should get. It was rather easy for them to refuse measures which would keep his body alive because they knew specifically what his wishes were. Paul's healthy level of Personal Death Awareness had permitted him to discuss his attitude toward extraordinary measures with his family. These conversations prevented misunderstandings or guilt feelings on their part.

In contrast to Paul, John never discussed the issue of prolonging his life with his two daughters. When his health declined to a point where he was unable to make decisions for himself, the question of using respirators and other life-sustaining devices was left up to these two sisters. Their father's health care became a battleground on which old sibling rivalries were rekindled. Each tried to outdo the other to see who could be the more attentive daughter. As a result, the elderly man, whose wife had died several years earlier and who had no hope for recovery, was kept alive much longer than was appropriate. If he had stated his preferences while still in relatively good health, he might have prevented the bad feelings that developed between his daughters and also the unnecessary prolongation of his life.

It may not be adequate just to talk with your loved ones about your wishes. It's easy for spoken words to be forgotten or distorted, and there's always a temptation to rationalize: "He didn't really mean that," or "He wasn't serious." To be certain your wishes are understood and followed, it's wise to put them down in writing. An increasingly popular method for doing this is through a document known as the "living will."[7]

If you become incapable of making decisions yourself, the living will can communicate your desires to family and others in charge of your care. This document is not legally binding, though a number of states have proposed statutes to make it a legal document. Here's a copy of a typical living will. Look it over and decide whether or not you'd want to sign it.

TO MY FAMILY, MY PHYSICIAN, MY CLERGYMAN, MY LAWYER

If the time comes when I can no longer take part in decisions for my own future, let this statement stand as the testament of my wishes:

If there is no reasonable expectation of my recovery from physical or mental disability,

I, _____

request that I be allowed to die and not be kept alive by artificial means or heroic measures. Death is as much a reality as birth, growth, maturity, and old age—it is the one certainty. I do not fear death as much as I fear the indignity of deterioration, dependence, and hopeless pain. I ask that medication be mercifully administered to me for terminal suffering even if it hastens the moment of death.

This request is made after careful consideration. Although this document is not legally binding, you who are for me will, I hope, feel morally bound to follow its mandate. I recognize that it places a heavy burden of responsibility upon you, and it is with the intention of sharing that responsibility and of mitigating any feelings of guilt that this statement is made.

Signed _____

Date _____
Witnessed by:

_____

_____

The Roman Catholic Church has drafted its own version of the living will:[8]

TO MY FAMILY, FRIENDS, PHYSICIAN, LAWYER, AND CLERGYMAN

I believe that each individual person is created by God our Father in love and that God retains a loving relationship to each person throughout human life and eternity.

I believe that Jesus Christ lived, suffered, and died for me and that his suffering, death, and resurrection prefigure and make possible the death-resurrection process which I now anticipate.

I believe that each person's worth and dignity derives from the relationship of love in Christ that God has for each individual person and not from one's usefulness or effectiveness in society.

I believe that God our Father has entrusted to me a shared dominion with him over my earthly existence so that I am bound to use ordinary means to preserve my life but I am free to refuse extraordinary means to prolong my life.

I believe that through death life is not taken away but merely changed, and though I may experience fear, suffering, and sorrow, by the grace of the Holy Spirit, I hope to accept death as a free human act which enables me to surrender this life and to be united with God for eternity.

BECAUSE OF MY BELIEF:

I request that I be informed as death approaches so that I may continue to prepare for the full encounter with Christ through the help of the sacraments and the consolation and prayers of my family and friends.

I request that, if possible, I be consulted concerning the medical procedures which might be used to prolong my life as death approaches. If I can no longer take part in decisions concerning my own future and if there is no reasonable expectation of my recovery from physical and mental disability, I request that no extraordinary means be used to prolong my life.

I request, though I wish to join my suffering to the suffering of Jesus so I may be united fully with him in the act of death-resurrection, that my pain, if unbearable, be alleviated. However, no means should be used with the intention of shortening my life.

I request, because I am a sinner and in need of reconciliation and because my faith, hope, and love may not overcome all fear and doubt, that my family, friends, and the whole Christian community join me in prayer and mortification as I prepare for the great personal act of dying.

Finally, I request that after my death, my family, my friends, and the whole Christian community pray for me, and rejoice with me because of the mercy and love of the Trinity, with whom I hope to be united for all eternity.

Signed ————————————————————— Date ————————————

Before you make a decision to sign either of these versions, look at a few objections that have been voiced against such documents.

Objection: There may be a last minute medical breakthrough on my illness, or I may recover unexpectedly.

Answer: Although it's unlikely scientists will come running over from a laboratory to save you, it is possible you might recover despite medical predictions to the contrary. Two cases of unexpected recoveries were reported in a special 1974 euthanasia issue of *Dimensions* published by Youville Hospital of Cambridge, Massachusetts.

In one case, a woman suffered a massive stroke and was not expected to live through the night. But she recovered and "lived twelve happy years beyond the time she was diagnosed as a hopeless invalid." In the other case, a young wife suffered a ruptured cerebral aneurysm and lay in a coma for months. Although her prognosis was poor, she improved sufficiently to be able to return home and live with her family for two rewarding years before she died.

Examples like these don't mean that it's unwise to give your family guidance through a living will. But they do mean it's important for your family to exhaust every reasonable medical possibility before deciding to take you off extraordinary support systems.

Objection: I might sign a living will and then change my mind.
Answer: To overcome this objection, advocates of the living will suggest that signers redate their wills once a year to affirm that their wishes have remained the same. If your desires change, you can alter the will accordingly.

Objection: After I've written down my orders in the living will, my family may decide not to follow them.
Answer: Regardless of whether you have a living will, your family may decide not to follow your wishes. But by putting your desires down on paper, there's a better chance that you can influence your family's decision.

Objection: The living will seems too loosely worded to cover the precise kinds of things I'm concerned about.
Answer: Write your own living will.

Several of these objections would carry more weight if the living will actually were a legal document that could be enforced in court. At present, however, it's only a guide or statement of your opinion which doesn't bind either your family or doctors to act in a certain way. Because so many medical ambiguities and emotional uncertainties can't be anticipated until the dying process actually begins, in the long run, perhaps it's best for the living will to remain in this nonlegal category.

Doctors and "death experts" talk freely about euthanasia, mercy killing, and extraordinary and ordinary measures of sustaining life. None of these concepts, however, are as clear-cut as their advocates or opponents suggest. Sometimes it's next to impossible to designate one tube running into a person's nose as an "ordinary" measure and another tube in his arm as "extraordinary."

At this point, I personally would prefer to have my family remove all life-sustaining systems if I were in an extreme, irreversible condition and if removing those devices would not create extra pain or discomfort. Like a long, serious conversation, the living will is just another way of informing your family about your wishes ahead of time. In the last analysis, after expressing our desires, you and I both have to trust our family and physicians, who may have the final responsibility to see that our end comes naturally and with dignity.

1. Nancy L. Caroline, "Dying in Academe," *The New Physician*, 21 (Nov., 1972), 654-657.
2. February 17, 1973.
3. Ibid.
4. "Who Shall Live and Who Shall Die," *Youville Hospital Dimensions*, 6(1974), 4.
5. Annette Caron, "A Hospital Administrator Reflects on Euthanasia," *Youville Hospital Dimensions*, 6(1974), 9.
6. James J. Gill, "Euthanasia: A Reflection on the Doctor and the Hospital," *Youville Hospital Dimensions*, 6(1974), 7.
7. Copies may be obtained from: Euthanasia Educational Council, 250 West 57th Street, New York, New York 10019.
8. Copies may be obtained from: The Catholic Hospital Association, St. Louis, Missouri 63104.

Chapter Ten

FREE TO CHOOSE WHERE

Death sometimes strikes without warning—a truck barreling toward you on the wrong side of the highway, a mugger with a nervous trigger finger, a tornado that swoops suddenly out of the sky and devastates your home. In these situations, we have no choice where we die. But many times death gives some premonition of its approach and provides us with the freedom to pick our last place.

In the past, before sophisticated hospital facilities developed, more people died at home, surrounded by family and friends. But with the establishment of intensive care units and medical technology which can extend life almost indefinitely, there has been a trend away from dying at home and toward dying in hospitals.

Better care in these institutions does not necessarily mean more humane care, or a more meaningful and dignified death. When death becomes inevitable, a comforting, supportive environment sometimes becomes more important than the immediate presence of extensive health care equipment.

So that you'll be in a better position to make an intelligent choice, take time now to explore some of the possible places where you could spend your last days. To get some perspective of what it's like to die in different locations, think of the places where some of your friends and relatives have died.

Person: (name)	In a hospital	At home	Nursing home	Other
1.	____	____	____	____
2.	____	____	____	____
3.	____	____	____	____
4.	____	____	____	____
5.	____	____	____	____

As you look over this list, try to remember which places seemed most conducive to a meaningful death. What factors made one

127

location better than another? Now consider your own preferences as you answer the following:

If I have a choice, I would prefer to die in _____
because _____

The most obvious place to die these days is in a *hospital.* According to recent estimates, about seventy percent of all Americans now die in some institution, many in hospitals. The main problem with dying in a hospital, however, is that they are oriented toward the cure of disease. If you're terminally ill, most hospitals will have fewer facilities and skilled workers to prepare you psychologically for a comfortable, dignified death.

Dying patients can be a frustration and embarrassment to hospital staffs dedicated to saving lives, rather than helping patients die. Doctors and nurses in such an environment tend to devote more time to patients who have a chance to recover and are thus more interesting, medically speaking. Some hospitals seem so eager to hide their dying patients that terminal cases are relegated to single rooms so they won't depress the morale of the other patients and medical staff.

There are notable exceptions to this tendency in hospitals to deny death. Youville, a Roman Catholic hospital in Cambridge, Massachusetts, and Calvary Hospital in the Bronx, are two institutions that offer sensitive care for the dying. Montreal's Royal Victoria Hospital opened a special section for dying patients in January, 1975, under the direction of Dr. Balfour Mount. This twelve-bed "Palliative Care Unit" offers care by an interdisciplinary health team, specially trained to meet the needs of the terminally ill and their families.

Because of the problems that accompany dying in a hospital, you may decide it would be much better to die at home. In one study, we asked a group of survivors whose relatives had died at home if they would also prefer to pass away in their own beds. The interviewees split almost fifty-fifty. Half were in favor of the idea, and the other half responded adamantly that "in no way" would they want to die at home.

One of the biggest difficulties they faced as survivors was that the room where their loved ones had died reminded them of the death. It was almost impossible to forget what had happened there. At one conference on death in which I participated, a colleague told me of his father who had died recently. The old man had actually collapsed on the floor of their den before anyone could rush him to the hospital.

"My mother still thinks she sees him lying on the rug whenever she walks into that room," the man said. "The scene upsets her so much that she stays out of the house most of the time. My brothers and I really get worried because we can never reach her on the phone."

Here are some other objections that the survivors we questioned expressed to the idea of having a loved one die at home:

"I felt helpless because I didn't think I could do enough for him. I wondered if he'd be better off in a hospital. . . ."

"By being around him all the time, I was too much aware of the progressive deterioration of his disease. It was almost unbearable, watching him go downhill hour by hour. . . ."

"She became so demanding that nothing I could do seemed to satisfy her. This made me angry, and then I felt guilty about my anger. . . ."

"I just couldn't take the incontinence. She soiled the bed continually. That was an embarrassment to her and made it very hard on me and the rest of the family. This problem would have been handled much better by the hospital staff. . . ."

Not everybody we interviewed was negative about the idea of dying at home. Here are some of the positive responses from the group of survivors we talked to:

"We were able to minister and care for him right up to the end. . . ."

"We could do more things for him. Once, we tried taking some of his favorite food into the hospital while he was staying there, but an angry nurse took it away!"

"Our whole family could be together while she was at home for those last few weeks. The kids were able to see that death was a natural part of life. It reminded me of stories I've heard about rural areas, where hospitals aren't easily accessible and families seem to be so much more closely knit. . . ."

Before you definitely decide you'd like to spend your last days at home, you should weigh the price your family will have to pay in terms of time and emotional and physical energy. As long as your medical care remains minimal, your home may be the best place. But as a practical matter, only about ten percent of those who say they want to die at home actually do. If the care required becomes too serious, it may be necessary to rely heavily on visiting nurses or to enter a hospital.

Staying at home would not be my choice if I were in severe pain, needed regular injections, became incontinent, or started wandering around the house without being aware of where I was.

A possible alternative to staying at your own home, especially if the need for nursing attention gets serious, is a *nursing or convalescent home*. These institutions can help with physical rehabilitation and are often set up to handle the long-term care of the elderly better than an individual family. But even these nursing homes have their limitations. Often they won't accept patients who have only a short time to live. Also, most are not equipped to give the additional physical and emotional support that dying patients need. When these nursing homes decide that a patient is terminal, they are likely to ship him off to a hospital.

In an effort to combine the best features of the hospital, home, and nursing home, some concerned experts on the problems of dying patients have established an institution known as the *hospice*. The international model for this concept is a place called St. Christopher's Hospice, just outside London. The dictionary defines a hospice as a place of refuge for travelers. The "travelers" at St. Christopher's and similar facilities are terminally-ill patients who are on their way to death.

Established as a Christian foundation in 1967, St. Christopher's, under the leadership of Dr. Cicely Saunders, has pioneered several new concepts in the care for the dying. The main emphasis is on establishing and maintaining meaningful human relationships. Individuals are encouraged to stay at home with their families and live as outpatients for as long as possible. They continue contacts with their loved ones even after they become full-time residents at the 54-bed facility.

Illnesses like pneumonia aren't treated too vigorously with respirators and other medical devices because the Hospice staff believes such machines can come between the patient and his family. Nor are Hospice residents hooked up to the tubes and intravenous feeding devices so common at hospitals. Instead, a strong patient may feed a weaker one with a spoon, even if the feeding takes a long time. This approach enables the sicker patient to maintain some sense of dignity; and the healthier person—even though he knows he's going to die—can feel more useful than would otherwise be possible.

One of the primary goals at St. Christopher's, mentioned in an earlier chapter, is pain management, to help the patients avoid a preoccupation with the discomfort of the dying process. Heroin is used in treating the pain, even though addiction may be the result. The medical staff reasons that most patients won't live long enough to be concerned about withdrawal from the drug. The staff also finds alcohol in social situations to be a helpful sedative for older patients. Each individual is expected to die, and the goal of all treatment is to assist them to that end in the most pleasant and comfortable way possible.

The social environment at St. Christopher's is enhanced by stressing a sense of community. Children of the staff members run about the gardens as part of an organized "playgroup," join the oldsters for lunch, and in general "bring the sounds of the beginning of life into our midst," Dr. Saunders says. There are few single rooms, and patients are encouraged to live together and engage in regular contact and conversation. Visiting hours are quite flexible, with no age restrictions on guests.

The emphasis on developing deep personal relationships "seems to be the way we are experiencing the life of Christ here and now," Dr. Saunders says. "He is often close to us in this work, for the place of weakness and death is His own chosen way. The glimpses of reconciliation and the new life which we see again and again are surely His Resurrection, made present once again for us all."

An American program similar to St. Christopher's has been started in Branford, Connecticut, outside New Haven. The staff at the Connecticut Hospice has defined the patient's family as the basic unit of care. Family members have been trained to participate in treatment along with the professional medical staff. When the facilities are completed, a wife or daughter may concentrate on cooking special meals for the patients both inside and outside the Hospice.

Families of patients will interact with one another in special facilities inside the Hospice, and family members can actually live inside the facility with their loved one when death becomes imminent.

A central concept of care at Hospice, as well as at St. Christopher's, is a service called the Home Care Team, which includes physicians, nurses, social workers, pastors, and various volunteers, helping patients live as long as possible in their own homes. The team members make from one to three visits every day to the home of each outpatient.

A good example of Home Care teamwork involved a fifty-seven-year-old woman who had a radical mastectomy of her left breast and was pronounced terminal by her doctor.[1] One Christmas Eve she began to experience severe pain which heat pads and drugstore remedies couldn't alleviate. Her family physician felt inadequate to help her overcome the despair she was feeling and asked the Hospice staff to take over treatment.

During the first home visit, the team nurse found her sitting immobilized in a darkened room. Pain and fear had interrupted her sleep and kept her housebound. She was sitting in front of a telephone, but hesitated to call her family because she was so frightened by her condition.

Through psychiatric consultations, collaboration with the Hospice pharmacists, and X-ray treatments, she improved and was able to enjoy a good night's rest. One of her favorite pastimes had been driving her car, but she had been afraid her legs would give out if she tried it again. After an examination by the Hospice staff showed her legs were strong enough, the team encouraged her to resume her driving.

Even though her life was drawing to a close, she found that her relationship with her family steadily improved. She got great satisfaction from splurging on a new dress for the 50th wedding anniversary party for her aunt and uncle. Mother's Day and the Fourth of July were extremely happy events for her. One Saturday evening, she attended just the kind of family gathering she had always enjoyed most: dinner with her entire brood, poker until midnight, and then a good night's sleep.

When her daughter looked in on her at nine o'clock the next morning, she was breathing easily and peacefully. At ten-thirty that same morning, she was dead.

This woman's experience with the Hospice home care program was far superior to what most hospitals can offer these days, and the cost of her treatment was considerably less. According to present estimates, it will cost about $108 per day to be treated at the Hospice during the fiscal year 1977. Treatment outside the Hospice through the Home Care program will be even less expensive, depending on the amount of treatment required. In contrast, general hospitals in Connecticut are expected to charge as much as $194 per day in fiscal 1977.[2]

Of course, your ability to choose a hospital, hospice, or nursing home may ultimately depend on the state of your finances. If you are like many people and have to rely on government support, such as Medicaid, you may find there are definite limits on the time you can stay in any of the facilities.

At present, I believe that the hospice is the best facility available to help dying patients, and such would be my choice. However, I don't think these institutions are the ultimate answer. Enough of them couldn't be established to meet the need. It seems more feasible to establish home care teams in our existing hospitals and educate the staff of these hospitals in the importance of setting up specific units to care for terminally-ill patients by using care principles similar to the hospice. This is exactly what the Royal Victoria Hospital in Montreal is trying to do. Hospitals can offer more complete medical facilities than hospices, and the cost, especially of home care programs, should be competitive with hospice rates. An ideal program would include not only spiritual and psychological counseling and medical treatment, but practical financial advice on insurance, attorney's fees, and funeral preparations.

But if such a home care program for dying people is to develop in our hospitals, present medical staffs must overcome their tendency to deny death and keep their Personal Death Awareness at ineffectually low levels. Straightforward, creative thinking will be necessary to come up with the comprehensive programs that are required to put our hospitals on a level with St. Christopher's, the Connecticut Hospice, and similar institutions.

1. Hospice (Brochure), Hospice, Incorporated, New Haven, Connecticut.
2. Ibid.

Chapter Eleven

FREE TO CELEBRATE LIFE

The tall, gray-haired man walked to the front of the funeral home chapel and cleared his throat. With an obvious effort to control his emotions, he announced, "Abby wrote this and she wanted you to hear it now."

Then he began to read: "Since no funeral is complete without some words about the departed, I feel it is not out of character to leave a personal message with you, my dear friends. Let this not be a day of sorrow but of thankfulness for a long life, devoted family and friends, a husband who has loved and enjoyed me for twenty-six years, and for my beloved sons to whom I now wish Godspeed wherever their lives shall take them.

"Farewell. No one can perceive the hereafter, but at least I believe firmly that 'by their works ye shall know them,' and all of us live on through the vessels we have created, the influences we have wrought, the lives we have touched. By this *credo*, death is not an end but a way station in the continuum of life, and tragic only if it cuts down a life unfulfilled. So join with me in my serenity, which it will be, when the pain is over. Mourn me briefly, then get on with the business of living, and let it be with a smile, the only thing I would wish for. God bless."[1]

Abby, a forty-nine-year-old woman who had died of breast cancer was one of a growing number of people with a healthy Personal Death Awareness who want to plan and participate in their own memorial services. When I suggested to a friend the idea of planning his own funeral service, he protested, "That's the last thing I'd want to do! Why on earth should I be interested in my funeral?"

"There are several good reasons," I told him. "The best way for me to explain is by example." Then I related the experience of three people who planned their own services and this man became more interested.

Esther   Before she died at age seventy-four, Esther decided she

134

wanted a traditional service in her home church with her minister presiding. Having been disabled by a stroke, she called her daughter aside one day and insisted that the younger woman listen to her wishes about her funeral. Despite protests like, "Oh, Mother, you're not going to die anytime soon!", the two finally got involved in a serious discussion. Esther jotted down some favorite hymns she wanted the church soloist and organist to render, including, "My Jesus I Love Thee," and "More Love to Thee O Christ." At the end of the service she wanted the entire congregation to sing her favorite gospel song, "When the Roll Is Called Up Yonder, I'll Be There." Another request was that the minister read several of her favorite Scriptures, including Paul's writings on Love and the resurrection of the body in I Corinthians 13 and 15; Jesus' teachings on heaven and how to get there in John 14; and the comforting words on death from Psalm 23.

Finally, Esther wrote several paragraphs which she put into a sealed envelope and asked one of her friends to read at the service. In the note she said, "I'm convinced that to be absent from the body is to be at home with the Lord. Death is a way to be reunited with members of my family who have already joined Him."

Because she had been so definite about her preferences, the service was conducted exactly as she had wished. Since she had asked that the funeral be conducted without a casket, her family substituted several of her watercolor paintings as a symbolic focus for the front of the sanctuary. Esther's favorite pastime had been cultivating roses, so her daughter gathered some from her garden and displayed them next to the paintings.

Esther had always been a happy, sociable sort of person, and her relatives and friends decided that it would be a nice touch to serve coffee and tea and provide some time for conversation after the service. Her faith, artistic interests, and friendliness had been so well integrated into the service that Esther's friends talked for weeks afterward about the appropriateness of her service.

Jeff   As an avid exponent of environmentalism and many of the counter-culture values of the 1960s, Jeff, a victim of leukemia, decided that he wanted to be cremated and then buried during an outdoor service. After he died, twenty of his friends chose a grassy meadow where Jeff had liked to hike. Sitting in a circle, they sang to the accompaniment of a guitar some of his favorite songs, including "Sunshine on My Shoulder" and "Everything Is Beautiful in Its Own Way."

In a kind of group eulogy, each person contributed some spontaneous comments about Jeff. Then, quietly and reverently, they opened a box containing his cremated remains and worked his ashes into the ground around the base of a huge oak tree. The service ended as the group with joined hands began to sing the Shaker song, "T'is a Gift to Be Simple," as they slowly circled the tree, which had become their friend's last marker.

John   John was a Scottish-born American who suffered a severe heart attack at age fifty, sensed he didn't have long to live, and he wanted to be sure that his memorial service was "not a bunch of nonsense." He loved many of the traditions of his native Scotland, but he had given up his religion and was adamant about not having a clergyman conduct his funeral.

"I want a kind of wake, where all my friends can look at me lying there, but I don't want it to be a snivelin' kind of thing," he told his sister. "After they take a look, they can shed a tear if they like, but then let's celebrate! A big dinner afterwards, with plenty of food and drink—that's what I want."

After he died, John's sister saw to it that his nonreligious wake was carried out just as he had directed. A funeral director conducted the service, and his eulogy was punctuated by recorded Scottish music and a reading from what John had called, "my favorite poet, old Bobby Burns."

As John's friends left the funeral home and headed toward the cemetery where he would finally be laid to rest, they knew that they would remember him not in some artificial, unnatural way, but as the vital, distinctive man he had been during his life.

In contrast to these three individuals, a beautiful, bikini-clad young woman I met at a swimming pool expressed an entirely different attitude. When I told her I was writing about planning your own funeral, she winced and said, "Why even think about that? When I'm dead, you can just dump me out beside the road. Why should I care what happens to my body?"

I didn't pursue the conversation at once, but I did take a closer look at her. She had obviously been working on a glorious tan, and apparently paid close attention to her diet and exercise. She was concerned, if not obsessed, about her physical attributes. I couldn't believe she would really want the body she spent so much time grooming to be "dumped." Before I could tell her why a funeral was important, she had left the lounge chair and executed a clean dive into the clear pool water. If she had stayed around a little longer, I might have given her three reasons for having a funeral.

1. Funerals help the people you leave behind affirm that you're really gone. Your friends and family members can't begin the grieving process unless they are convinced you're dead. The funeral service helps them establish in their minds the fact that you really are dead, and not just "away."
2. A funeral facilitates the grieving process. Grieving is essentially a recognition that your survivors have sustained a loss and must express sadness, anger, or other feelings that go with such a loss. Grief also marks the beginning of emotional withdrawal from the deceased so that your energy can be invested in those who are still living. Without an adequate period of grieving, a person may get stuck emotionally, and find it hard to let go of the lost one and form new relationships.
3. Finally, funerals provide your survivors with a socially acceptable ritual to dispose of your body. In our society, the funeral industry has taken over the supervision of this function and has eliminated the need for family members or friends to perform the function of burial.

There's no doubt that some kind of funeral is necessary from a purely practical point of view. But you may ask, "Is there really any reason for me to take time *now* to plan my own funeral? Why not just let my survivors worry about that?"

Let me suggest several distinct advantages:

First, planning your memorial service gives you a chance to participate in the final event of your life—your farewell. It's very hard for our minds to grasp what it will be like to be alive no longer. These sentiments were in the mind of the poet Ted Rosenthal when he entitled a book of poems, *How Could I Not Be*

Among You? Preparing your service allows you in a sense *to be there*, in absentia, to say good-bye.

Second, prior planning assures you that things which were important to you during your lifetime will be emphasized. It is possible that these things would be emphasized even if you did nothing, but stating your preferences leaves little to chance. Should your death occur suddenly, the shock of such a loss often makes it difficult for family members to plan a service adequately.

Finally, planning your service in advance will make your family feel more comfortable when attending to final details like the choice of a casket, flowers, and the size of the ceremony. Families who have no guidance must fall back on speculation: "I think he would have wanted this, but maybe. . . ." It's better to bring the subject up now and not leave them in doubt. Just say, "I definitely don't want any flowers," or "I would prefer a closed casket," or "I would really be disappointed if you bought an expensive coffin."

At this point take a few minutes and consider what might be an appropriate service to celebrate your life after you are gone. I realize that this is not an easy task, but doing it can put you in touch with some important thoughts and feelings.

I would like my service to take place:

_____ in my church or synagogue.
_____ at home.
_____ at a funeral chapel.
_____ outdoors.
_____ at the graveside only.
_____ other: _____

Most funerals take place in funeral homes, but some services, especially those involving Roman Catholics and members of certain evangelical Christian groups, are held in churches. Jewish funerals are frequently conducted in a funeral home or at the cemetery. It's also possible to have a ceremony at your home, though this choice may be difficult for your family.

Wherever you decide to have the service, the service should reflect you—*your* uniqueness. Since it will be a time of remembering and recollection, what would you most like people to remember about you? Think about this and make some notes.

What I want people to remember about me:

My interest in: _____

_____

_____

My traits of: _____

_____

_____

My accomplishments: _____

_____

_____

Now consider some procedural issues. Somebody will have to convene the service. Who would you like to do this?

I would like the following person to officiate at my service:

_____ my clergyman: _____
_____ my funeral director: _____
_____ a psychologist: _____
_____ a friend: _____
_____ a family member: _____
_____ other: _____

Many people think it's essential to have a member of the clergy lead a funeral. Not so! Although the clergy are most frequently in charge, it's not essential that an ordained person even participate, let alone officiate. Understanding this fact may be a relief to you if you're not particularly religious or active in the institutional church.

If you are reluctant to have a minister or rabbi in charge, your local funeral director is probably highly qualified and experienced, both in preparing and chairing services. It's also quite acceptable to choose a qualified family member. I was invited to officiate at my grandfather's service, and I think my presence helped contribute a personal element that would have been absent otherwise.

Because of the intensity of emotion that may grip close family members after your death, it may be hard for them to participate publicly in your service. Your friends may be in a better position to contribute something to your final celebration.

Here are the names of friends that I'd like to have participate in my service:

1. _____

2. _____

3. _____

4. _____

5. _____

Think of a specific function for each person. Ways they might participate are:

If you had trouble thinking of things your friends might do, let me suggest a few possibilities. Some might act as pallbearers. Others might offer prayers, read poetry or Scripture, and perhaps even give a short talk or eulogy. One or two could play or sing musical selections. You may prefer to have a brief time set aside for those with special thoughts on their minds to make spontaneous comments of remembrance. Finally, there could be opportunity for others to help prepare food or to serve as ushers.

Now think about the service itself—what you would like it to include:

Some specific things I'd like to have included in my service are:

Music:

Poetry:

Scriptures:

Other readings:

Other features (such as interpretive dance, art forms, etc.):

In considering readings and creative presentations for your service, you are choosing material which reflects those things which are important to you. The manner of expressing these beliefs and convictions is limited only by your imagination and sense of taste. I recently attended a memorial service where three persons in the chapel read antiphonally a series of brief statements which had been written by the deceased.

Your convictions may include your beliefs as to the meaning of your life and death, where you came from and where you are going. Some people focus on beliefs which sustain them and enable them to function when life gets very rough. If you believe that your life has a plan and purpose, share this with those who will be joining in the celebration of your life.

Religious or philosophical convictions I want expressed in the service:

Perhaps you might want to write a draft of your own final message as Abby did. Look again at her letter in the beginning of this chapter.

A statement which I would like read:

Up to this point, we've dwelt on the positive things to be included in your service. Undoubtedly there are some things you *don't* want included. I believe most people have had one or two bad experiences which create strong negative reactions at the thought of attending funerals. Here are a few examples:

• For Earl, it was the minister who gave an altar call and made everyone present feel guilty and disrespectful to the dead man unless they came forward and made some commitment of faith.

• For Mary, it was having to kiss the body of her grandmother. When she was a small child, her mother insisted that she do it, and Mary became quite frightened.

• For Fred, it was the insincere comments he heard at his brother's service. Fred's brother had been a selfish person who had mistreated his family. But these deficiencies were ignored while excessive, false praise echoed from one corner of the funeral chapel to the other.

• For Charlie, it was the way they made his elderly dad look bigger and better than life. The funeral cosmetician had removed all the wrinkles which had given his father character.

Things I definitely do *not* want at my service:

In listing the things you don't want at your funeral, you may have said you object strongly to having anyone view your dead body. This is a difficult decision, and personally I have very mixed feelings about it. On the one hand, I believe it is deceptive to fix up the body to make it look more lifelike. This practice makes it harder for the family to accept the death and to overcome the denial that it has occurred. Psychologically speaking, to say or imply through cosmetics, "She's only sleeping," can do more harm than good.

On the other hand, it may be helpful and even necessary for someone to view your body—to identify you if you've been killed in an accident, for example. Also, if your loved ones don't see you to ascertain that you are the one who is dead, they may be reluctant to accept your loss as real. Consciously or subconsciously, they may convince themselves that you're just away and will be back again.

Many ethnic, cultural, and geographic factors determine how you feel about having your family and friends view your body. My own preference would be to have my immediate family view my body unless I were severely disfigured. But I'd like my casket to be closed or to have no casket at the funeral service. It can be quite appropriate in place of a casket to have a personal photograph, painting, floral display, military medals, or any other symbols of your life.

As you try to reach a decision about viewing, it's important to keep the sensitivities of your family in mind. In the last analysis, *they* are the ones who will be affected most by this decision. If they feel strongly they'd rather remember you as you were alive and not view your dead body, then perhaps their attitudes should be the controlling consideration.

In addition to the memorial service, some decisions will have to be made about what to do with your body. You can choose to leave these decisions up to your family, or you can think about them now, discuss them, and come to some resolution while you are still alive.

There are several advantages in confronting these issues before you die. First, if you do consider the alternatives and make some choices, you can insure that your preference will be carried out. Second, preplanning can insure that the costs to your survivors will be kept within a range that you consider reasonable. Families who make such decisions in the midst of grief, without having given them prior consideration, tend to spend more on funerals and arrangements than those who have thought these issues through.

Here are the major decisions relating to the disposition of your body:

Decision 1—Cremation or Burial

Your first important decision is whether to be buried or cremated. The age-old custom of cremation is becoming the choice for a greater number of Americans every year, especially on the West Coast. In cremation your body is placed in a container and then burned in a retort or special furnace for about two hours. At the end of this period, all that remains is small bone fragments and ashes. The oven will cool after another two hours. Then the attendants will collect the ashes and place them in a small cardboard box, or a decorative urn of your choice. The cremation can take place before or after the funeral, so your body can be present at a memorial service if you like.

Several things may be done with your ashes. One option is to have them scattered, but laws on this practice vary from state to state. Some states, for example, want to know on the burial permit exactly where the ashes have been deposited. A few people choose to have their ashes scattered out of an airplane over the ocean, a forest, or some other place which has special meaning for them. Others prefer to have their remains put into an urn and kept in the home of a willing survivor or in a special place at the cemetery known as a colombarium—a building with numerous niches for the storing of the cremation urns. It's also possible for your ashes to be buried, either with or without a marker to identify the location.

The costs of cremation tend to be less than for burial because there's no need for an expensive casket, ground liners, plot costs, or opening and closing costs. Most crematoria require a suitable container to house the body during cremation, but it's not necessary to have a casket for this purpose. Cremation costs, at this writing, generally run about $80 to $480, with considerable variations from place to place.

The urns usually look like a closed vase or a large jewel box and measure about a foot high. They can be made of substances like bronze, silver, or marble. The cost, which depends on the choice of material, varies from $50 to several thousand dollars. Cemeteries usually make more profit from the sale of the urns than they do from the cost of the cremation. If you expect your remains to be shipped from one part of the country to another, the cost will be less with an urn than with a casketed body.

In addition to the low cost, cremation has several other advantages. It's quick and clean, and the body is not subject to the usual organic deterioration which always occurs in burial, no matter how well sealed or expensive your casket is. Ashes also take up much less room than the burial of a casket or entombment in a mausoleum. This compactness is becoming a major advantage in our era of overpopulation and increasing need for land in urban areas. I doubt, however, that people choose cremation for ecological reasons.

Most religious traditions, except for certain Orthodox Jewish sects, condone cremation. On May 8, 1963, for example, Pope Paul VI said, "Cremation may be permitted for serious reasons, of a private as well as public nature, provided it does not involve any contempt of the church. . . . A priest may say prayers for the deceased at the crematorium, but full liturgical ceremonies may not take place there."

Decision 2—The Casket

Although cremation has been gaining popularity, traditional burial in a casket is still the most common way of disposing of your body. If you opt for burial, you will be faced with a second decision—a container.

In old days, bodies were dropped into the ground or placed in simple pine boxes before being buried. Today, you can get caskets made of anything from corrugated cardboard and wood to fine metals such as bronze and copper. Caskets have traditionally been a large expense item in the funeral budget—an item which adds greatly to the funeral director's profit. Walk into the display room of the average funeral home and you'll be confronted by a bewildering array of coffins of every imaginable size, shape, and texture. You'll see gleaming blue and bronze containers with inner linings of silk and satin and special caskets that can be made airtight to delay the inevitable deterioration of your body.

A friend of mine walked into just such a room the day after his father died. But he was more prepared than most people to make an intelligent choice. On several occasions his father had stressed, "I don't want you to spend a lot of money on my funeral. An old pine box is all I need."

Armed with this understanding of his late father's wishes, my friend entered that funeral home knowing just what he wanted. As the funeral director led him into the display room, he was immediately confronted by twenty or thirty coffins, with the most expensive and ostentatious placed nearest the door. Had he been forced to speculate about what his father would have wanted, it could have been a very confusing and embarrassing experience. Think about how hard it would be, after *your* loved one is gone, to say to a stranger—even if you know he's only interested in selling you a coffin—"I want the cheapest thing you have."

But my friend could say with assurance, "My dad said he wanted a simple pine box, and I want the closest thing you have to that."

"We don't carry pine boxes any more," the funeral director replied.

"Anything in wood?" my friend persisted.

"Well, yes, back this way."

They walked to a side room that the young man would never have known about if he hadn't asked questions. In that small alcove he found three wooden caskets. They were covered tastefully in a fabric that made them look much like some of the coffins in the main room that cost five times as much.

"It was almost an exhilarating feeling to be able to walk into a situation like that," my friend told me afterward, "I knew I was making a choice that would leave several thousand dollars in my mother's hands and at the same time fulfill my dad's deep-seated desire."

I myself believe there's a great deal to be said for a simple, inexpensive casket. After all, no one will be able to admire a container buried in the ground. But this is a very personal issue that you have to decide for yourself. And you can decide *now* and help your family through a difficult later decision.

Decision 3—Embalming

In most states, embalming of your body is not required by law, but it's important both for aesthetic and sanitary reasons. Most funeral directors highly encourage it because of the rapid body deterioration which occurs after death.

In embalming, the blood and other bodily liquids are drained off and replaced by a fluid which retards the deterioration of tissue and prevents the odor of decomposition. This procedure is essential if the body is going to be available for viewing before, during, or after the memorial service. If the body is not going to be viewed, or if you plan cremation, embalming isn't as necessary. One alternative is refrigeration, which can keep the body "fresh" for a long period of time. But refrigeration is not as efficient and cheap as embalming and isn't available at every funeral establishment.

Decision 4—Place of Burial

The most common resting place for a casket is underneath the earth in an established cemetery. If you want to be buried in your own backyard, you may run into difficulty. Most cities and towns have zoning regulations for burials, and your yard is probably not included among permissible burial sites. If you live in a rural area, though, it's more likely you can choose to end up under the old apple tree.

If you decide on a cemetery plot, you can find one by looking in the Yellow Pages of your phone book or, better yet, by asking a friend who has had the experience of buying a plot of his own. In some parts of the country, door-to-door salesmen come around peddling lots, but it's risky to make such an important purchase sight unseen.

The price of the plot is determined by location and size. Sites which are easily accessible or have a particularly scenic view tend to go for more money. You'll also pay more if you buy a large plot, but if you want to have all your family buried nearby, it may be advisable to buy several plots together. Many families, including my own, have space in a cemetery which has been passed down from generation to generation because of the foresight of one ancient and honorable forebear. But there are dangers in too much foresight. A friend whose relatives also place great value on being prepared told me that his family has more plots than they can possibly use. Several concerned relatives have bought multiple plots in various locations, but since neither my friend nor his siblings have children, he expects that most of the plots will remain vacant.

If you buy a plot and then decide you want to sell it later, the cemetery association will buy it back at the original price. Sometimes the cemetery will let you sell to another private individual, but the cemetery officials frequently must approve your choice of a buyer. In the past, there were many more restrictions than there are now on who could be buried in a particular spot. Even if religious and ethnic restrictions weren't written down, they were definitely understood.

If you move to another part of the country, you don't need to sell your old plot. Instead, you can swap it for another in your new location under a program set up by the National Association of Cemeteries. The only problem with this arrangement is that your new town may have more expensive lots and you'll have to pay the difference in price. Still, I think this exchange policy is a good thing; it accommodates the high rate of mobility in our society and can encourage a sense of continuity after you move. If you'd prefer to keep your original cemetery plot for sentimental reasons, you can have your body or ashes shipped back to your original home. Airlines provide special rates for this service.

A number of innovative trends in modern cemeteries are eliminating many of the depressing, macabre aspects of burial. Forest Lawn Memorial Park began as one park, but now includes several facilities in Southern California. These parks, the dream of Colonel Eaton, offer mortuary services as well as cemetery and columbarium space. All grave markers at Forest Lawn must be level with the ground. To my mind this requirement not only preserves the natural beauty of the park, but also in some sense equalizes the graves of the rich and the poor.

The existence of a number of chapels enables the funeral officials to conduct simultaneously several funerals and sometimes even a wedding or two. These parks have been satirized by Johnny Carson on his television show and by Evelyn Waugh in his book *The Loved One,* but I think such facilities represent a movement toward a healthier attitude about death. The artwork and architecture of the chapels may not always be harmonious with the California landscape, but on the whole, the parks are well-planned and offer families full funeral services in a beautiful natural setting.

Another burial concept is the mausoleum where casketed bodies are stored above ground in appropriate buildings. Currently, a high-rise version of a mausoleum is being built in Nashville, Tennessee. Land availability and increasing real estate costs make this type of facility attractive in highly congested urban centers. Some people object to this trend, however, because of the impersonal qualities often associated with high-rise office buildings.

There are several other considerations you should keep in mind as you calculate potential burial costs. Your family won't have to worry about upkeep on your grave because, through endowment funds, most cemeteries provide what they call "perpetual care" as part of the original price. But your survivors will be assessed "opening and closing costs" at the time of your burial. These terms are a fancy way of describing the digging of a hole for your casket, filling it in after the ceremony, and replacing the grass on top of the grave.

Another expense is the grave liner—usually a cement box which costs roughly $85 to $100. Practically all cemeteries require that a liner be used because it keeps the ground from caving in after the casket deteriorates. An alternative to the liner is a metal or stone vault buried in the ground. These vaults can keep your casket dry and sealed off from the air and thus satisfy the needs of some who want to have their bodies preserved underground as long as possible. If you are buried in a cemetery which doesn't require a liner or vault and you want to avoid this extra expense, your grave can be filled in with new soil after the appearance of surface indentations indicates the casket underneath has caved in.

Despite the romantic or mysterious aura that surrounds the "unmarked grave," most people want some kind of a marker, and I think it's wise to provide for one. It's important in the grieving process for survivors to have a place where they can go and remember the deceased. I've counseled people who had lost a loved one but had no marker which established for them the fact of death. Some of these people have had difficulty resolving their grief because of the lack of a concrete symbol which could help them remember the loss and then release their emotional hold on the deceased.

Markers range from a simple slab at ground level to large and ornate tombstones. They can add substantially to the cost of being buried, but it's also possible to find less expensive stones that serve just as well as tremendous monuments. I noticed recently in a Sears store near my home that a department had been set up between the stereos and draperies to sell memorial tablets. I say, "More power to Sears!" Putting such funeral items on the open market can only be helpful as people try to face death as a fact of life. There is a large profit markup on memorial markers, however, so don't settle on the first one you see. Shop around for the best price, just as you'd shop around for a new television set.

Many of these funeral choices—including the casket, cemetery plot, and marker—can be had for a relatively small amount of money. It's also possible to turn your funeral into a Cecil B. DeMille extravaganza and invest thousands of dollars in the process. Funeral costs can run as low as nothing if you're on welfare, to as much as several thousand dollars if you are rich—or if you allow yourself to die as though you're rich.

The possibility of spending too much money has provoked criticisms of excessive profit-making against the funeral industry from authors like Jessica Mitford and has prompted a recent investigation by the Federal Trade Commission. Some of the criticisms are justified, but it's also important to remember that funeral directors are running a business and providing services that cost money. If you pick an enlightened funeral director who sees his work as a calling or profession, his services at a time of great need and sorrow can be well worth the cost. On the other hand, if you let yourself be gouged because of a lack of forethought, that's your fault as much as the funeral director's.

Every profession has its incompetents, and funeral directors are no exception. But many morticians, especially those trained by organizations like the Uniservice Corporation of Oregon, are able to offer significant skilled counseling to families at the time of grief. These funeral specialists are being instructed in psychology and sensitivity training—not to fill their pockets, but to help you and your family. A well-trained mortician can often do as much as a minister or psychologist to facilitate the grieving process.

Even at your own funeral, you are the buyer and you don't have to buy blindly. Increase your Personal Death Awareness now so that you can examine the options intelligently. Take the initiative to inquire about possible services and decide definitely what you want. The best way to relieve any anxieties or uncertainties you may feel about your memorial service is to take action. Make a list of all the things you want your final celebration to include. Then have your lawyer insert your wishes into your will, or give written instructions to a trusted friend or relative. Your family won't be ripped off or confused unless you make the mistake of allowing them to be.

1. Ruth D. Abrams, *Not Alone With Cancer* (Springfield, Illinois: Charles C. Thomas, 1974), 85.

IV

Changing
Your
Life Span

Chapter Twelve

FREE TO EXTEND LIFE

We have no control over when our death occurs. "When your time comes, it comes, and there's nothing you can do about it!" a patient told me one day. This notion is quite common—but not entirely true. There are many kinds of death over which you have no control. But sometimes you can affect the inner time clock that determines your life span, and extend or shorten your life for significant periods. The book of Ecclesiastes says, "To everything there is a season and a time to every purpose under heaven . . . a time to be born and a time to die." The season or time of your death depends not only on God or fate, but also on your attitude toward your own life and mortality.

First of all, your outlook on life can hasten your death without your even being aware of it. A dramatic example of life shortened by emotions is sudden voodoo death, which occurs among some primitive peoples as the result of a hex or curse. Dr. R. J. W. Burrell of the Bantu Cancer Registry in Capetown, South Africa, described an incident of this type at a medical meeting in Detroit.[1]

"I saw an old woman cast a spell on a man," he recalled. "She said, 'You will die before sunset.' And he did. The man believed he was going to die, and he jolly well died. At autopsy, no cause of death could be found."

Halfway around the world at the Melanoma Clinic in New South Wales, Australia, G. W. Milton told about another voodoo death that involved an aborigine tracker named "Big Paddy."[2] This tracker had worked for the police for twenty-five years in a small, isolated western Australian town. He appeared to have become completely integrated into modern society. But his deep-rooted beliefs in witchcraft surfaced while he was out on a patrol with two other black trackers and a white police officer.

The group surprised a tribe which was thought to have been responsible for a murder, and the tribe's witch doctor cursed Big Paddy and the other invaders. All three aborigines knew they had been cursed, but Paddy seemed to be more affected than his companions. In less than twenty-four hours, he began to show complete indifference to everything around him. He remained in the saddle for the rest of the patrol mission, but he ignored every remark or gesture directed toward him.

Big Paddy didn't seem to be shaking with fear, but he was completely cut off from his surroundings. He refused even to look at his white companion and was uninterested in eating his food. Despite all efforts to reach him, he became weaker and more withdrawn. He finally died a few weeks later.

Big Paddy and other victims of voodoo have succumbed to the power of such curses because they *believe* there is a power which is destroying them. Where there is no belief, the person remains unaffected.

Some medical experts have detected a similarity between these reactions to voodoo curses and the diagnosis of a terminal disease.[3] In voodoo, after the victim is cursed, everyone in the community withdraws from him, and he, in turn, withdraws from the community. Having severed all social and psychic bonds, the person accepts death as preferable to complete isolation and ostracism. In a modern hospital, after a patient's illness is diagnosed as a terminal disease, the medical staff often withdraws from him and hides behind their impersonal facade as health care professionals. The sick person's family may also withdraw into silence, denial, or superficial cheerfulness.

In a classic case illustrating the emotional power of such a diagnosis, as a result of an incorrect reading of an X-ray, a patient was mistakenly told that he had lung cancer. After the diagnosis the man became much sicker. He lost weight, became depressed, and developed chest pains and a cough. But when informed that the original diagnosis was wrong, even before he received any additional treatment, he began to show remarkable physical and emotional improvement. Drs. Thomas Hackett and Avery Weisman, who studied this patient's case in detail, concluded that the initial diagnosis of lung cancer became a kind of hex which left the man feeling helpless and hopeless.[4]

Whether a hex is put on you by a doctor in a hospital or by natives in a primitive society, the important thing is your belief that you are doomed. If the patient in Hackett and Weisman's study had ignored the unfavorable diagnosis, it's likely his health would never have declined. And if Big Paddy had shrugged off the witch doctor's curse, he might still be alive today.

If you begin to believe that your days are numbered and give in to the threat of helplessness and hopelessness, you may well be headed for a premature grave. Dr. George Engel of the University of Rochester School of Medicine has done considerable research on people who have died in situations where there seemed to be no usual medical reason for them to die.[6] He has found that a large percentage died either shortly after hearing about the death of a loved one, or after literally being scared to death.

The common thread running through these deaths is that the victim felt powerless to do anything about his environment. Life had become unbearable because of the loss of the loved one, or too threatening because of the danger which was bearing down. The individual becomes overwhelmed by what Engel calls a sense of "psychological impotence," and just gives up.

You may want to keep an eye out for the following characteristics which Engel has identified in those who have given up on life. Reverse this type of outlook in yourself, and you may avoid a self-imposed curse which can possibly hasten you to a premature death.

1. Sensing that you are at the end of your rope, you feel *helpless* and unable to influence your environment. You begin to believe everything is hopeless; no person or thing is able to save you.
2. The inability to affect your environment makes you feel *worthless*. You start saying, or thinking, "I'm no good and not worth saving."
3. Your job, hobbies, and relationships with other people *no longer gratify* you. Nothing seems interesting or exciting any more.
4. You think you're isolated in the present and there is *no continuity* any more between your past, present, and future. You find it hard to project yourself into the future through planning or aspiring toward some goal.
5. Finally, your mind becomes filled with *memories or events in your past* life which involved feelings of helplessness and hopelessness similar to those you're experiencing now.

I've encountered some elderly people who have been discharged from a hospital to nursing homes known to handle terminally-ill cases. These patients soon begin to exhibit symptoms of giving up on life. Sarah, a woman with advanced cancer, seemed quite lively and interested in improving her condition when I worked with her in the hospital. But when she got well enough to move to the nursing home, she became indifferent to everything around her. She died shortly after her transfer to the home, well before the doctors had predicted that she might die. I'm convinced that the primary reason for her untimely death was that she had decided that life wasn't worth living any longer.

Before her death, Sarah said to us several times, "I'm not going to be around much longer," and, "This is the last time you'll see me." These were not suicidal statements, but rather revealed a phenomenon common to many seriously ill people—the prediction of the time of death. Certainly many premonitions of death are not forecasts of what is to come, but are simply ploys to get the medical staff to pay more attention. But some premonitions actually come true. Robert Kastenbaum, who has studied these premonitions, says, "Some death premonitions are authentic forecasts of impending terminality, even though information from the usual channels would not predict imminent death. The patient knows before the medical establishment does."[6]

Kastenbaum has noticed that patients can also communicate their impending death through nonverbal signs. A significant reduction in anxiety, for example, may signal a lack of concern about life and a readiness to give up.

In our study of cancer patients at the Omega Project, we tried to determine why certain people survive longer than medical experts expect, and why other individuals live for unusually short periods. We found that patients who live significantly longer tend to maintain meaningful personal relationships, especially as the end of life draws near. In contrast, people with death wishes, depressions, apathy, and unsatisfying personal relationships die sooner than they should.[7,8]

People who last for the longest periods seem to have the most to live for. They refuse to accept the fact that death is inevitable, and their life spans stretch out accordingly. Some deny the gravity of their illnesses, and most fight the gradual deterioration of their bodies. The fight they wage seems to arrest the dying process.[9]

On the other hand, most of those who die weeks or months before the medical staff expects have a long history of poor social relationships, sometimes including early separations as children from their families. Frequently they suffer from obvious psychiatric disorders, and many seem to dwell on the destructive dealings they've had with others. On occasion, they've considered suicide. When they learn their medical treatment has failed, instead of fighting against their inevitable death, they give up. They become more depressed and highly pessimistic, and express a desire to die.[10]

My observation of dying patients has convinced me that you *can* extend your life if your will to live is strong enough. It is common to find sick people who have lived months beyond medical expectations because they want to make it to a date that has special meaning for them. The date may involve the wedding of a son or daughter, a birthday, or an anniversary. For instance, two of our founding fathers and former presidents, John Adams and Thomas Jefferson, died on July Fourth.

One of the most remarkable stories of a person living far beyond medical predictions was related to me by Bob Reeves, a chaplain at Columbia Presbyterian Hospital in New York City.[11] A friend of his, dying of cancer, told him it was very important for her to live to see the New Year, which was still several months away. She even bet Bob a dollar she would live until the New Year. Happy that she was able to face the subject of her own death so naturally, he accepted her challenge, but neither of them informed the other family members of the wager.

On New Year's Eve, Bob spent the evening with this woman's family. At the stroke of midnight, everyone raised glasses in a toast to the New Year. The sick woman, who was sitting in the family circle in her wheelchair, held out her hand to Bob, and she smiled as he reached into his pocket and handed her a dollar bill. She accepted it, grasped it tightly, folded her hands, and died.

She had kept herself alive through the strength and force of her spirit, and lengthened her life until she reached that final deadline she had set for herself.

Sometimes the will to live can be wrapped up in the sick person's sense of responsibility toward his family. One autumn we saw a young mother who had a terminal case of cancer. After she learned that her condition was rapidly getting worse and that she might not live past the end of the year, we could almost see the willpower surge up in her.

Thinking of her small children, she declared, "I'll be damned if I'll die at Christmas and always have my kids associate that happy holiday with my death."

We were amazed as we watched her struggle past the Christmas season with tremendous determination and fortitude. January had almost come to a close when she finally died.

Up to this point, we've assumed that it's a good thing to extend life and a bad thing to shorten it. It is possible to live too long, however. Sometimes a sick person may actually want to die, but he may be afraid to let go and face death. His struggle against death keeps him alive, even though he's supremely unhappy and dissatisfied with his condition.

Dr. Eric Cassell of the Cornell Medical Center sees death as a process in which the dying person can play a part, both to extend *and* to shorten his life, whichever seems appropriate.[12] Cassell has found that when he gives a person permission to die, "the patient becomes more peaceful and . . . pain, if present, becomes less severe and more bearable, and . . . within a relatively short time, the patient dies."[13]

It's a difficult and controversial decision for a physician to tell a patient to quit fighting and let death take over. Although Cassell sees this opening of the door to death as a valid function in the physician's role with a dying patient, I would be cautious in encouraging family members to do this. A sense of guilt and personal responsibility after the death may be difficult to overcome.

Much of the research into the will to live and will to die is inconclusive at this point, but it's clear to me that the human spirit has considerable power to hasten or postpone the moment of death. If you're emotionally stable—free of excessive anxiety and depression—and if your relationships with other people are generally meaningful, you'll probably prefer to stay on this earth as long as you can. By *wanting* to live, even if you are very ill, you may be able to extend your life for weeks or even months beyond what your doctors expect.

1. R.J.W. Burell, "Spells, Sorcery and the Will to Die," *Medical World News*, 25(1961), 33.

2. G.W. Milton, "Self-Willed Death or the Bone-Pointing Syndrome," *Lancet* (June 23, 1973), 1435-1436.
3. Thomas P. Hackett and Avery D. Weisman, "Hexing in Modern Medicine," *Proceedings of the 3d World Congress of Psychiatry.* (Montreal: McGill Univ. Press, 1961), 1249-1252.
4. Ibid.
5. George Engle, "A Psychological Setting of Somatic Disease: The 'Given Up—Giving Up' Complex," *Proceedings of Royal Society of Medicine,* 60(1967), 1-3.
6. Robert Kastenbaum, "Premonitions of Death and Their Implications for Psychological Intervention." Mimeographed manuscript.
7. Avery D. Weisman and J.W. Worden, "Psychosocial Analysis of Cancer Deaths," *Omega,* 6 (1975), 61-75.
8. J. W. Worden, L.C. Johnston, R.H. Harrison, Survival Quotient as a Method for Investigating Psychosocial Aspects of Cancer Survival, *Psychological Reports,* 35(1974), 719-726.
9. Ibid.
10. Ibid.
11. Robert Reeves, Personal communication.
12. Eric Cassell, "Permission to Die," *Bioscience,* 23(1973), 475-478.
13. Ibid.

Chapter Thirteen

FREE TO END LIFE

"I wish I were dead!"

How often did you utter these words as a child? As an adult, has the thought of killing yourself ever crossed your mind? In previous chapters we've discussed a number of possible choices you have about the way to die. Now we come to the ultimate choice, the choice to die by your own hand—the choice of suicide. Most people have thought about ending their own lives at one time or another. You may have thought about it yourself, but not realized how common the experience is.

I once was invited to discuss suicide on a national television program. During the interview I mentioned in passing that a majority of people have considered suicide at least once in their lives.

The deluge of mail I received had a common theme: "Thank you for telling me how common self-destructive thoughts are." Many of these viewers said they had been oppressed by the idea that these thoughts were unique. They had never shared their suicidal thoughts with anyone, not even close relatives.

Some experts think that the ability to entertain suicidal thoughts is what keeps many people sane—and alive. I share that opinion. Most of us don't opt for self-destruction, but knowing that it's a possibility can be a comforting thought. Nietzsche once remarked that, "the thought of suicide is a great consolation; by means of it one gets successfully through many a bad night."[1] And psychologist Rollo May has declared, "I am doubtful whether anyone takes [considers] his life with full seriousness until he realizes that it is entirely within his power to commit suicide."[2]

Recall a situation where you were plagued by some great unhappiness, such as the loss of a loved one or losing your job. Do you think your stress might have been eased if you had *considered* killing yourself? Psychiatrist Rudolph Reitler has written that the mere idea that profound anxiety can be ended once and for all seems to have such a comforting effect that it's possible

many people may be kept alive only by their suicidal fantasies.[3]
Stop for a minute and check one of the following statements
which best describes yourself.

_____ I have never had a suicidal thought.
_____ I have occasionally had suicidal thoughts.
_____ I constantly have suicidal thoughts.
_____ I have self-destructive thoughts and have threatened
suicide by communicating these thoughts to others.
_____ I have had such thoughts and have actually made a sui-
cidal attempt.

Although most people who consider suicide don't actually kill
themselves, a significant minority do decide to take their own
lives. There are approximately 25,000 to 30,000 suicide deaths
reported in this country every year. Many observers estimate that
the number of suicides that go unreported would raise these
figures to a much higher level. Our studies, for example, show that
for one reason or another, a number of suicides get recorded as
accidental deaths.

Who are these people who end up killing themselves? Are they
crazy? Some are, if you take "crazy" to mean "psychotic," but
others are not. In other words, it's not necessary to be insane to
kill yourself. Nor is there any single suicide-prone type of person.
People of all ages, occupations, sexes and social classes kill
themselves.

There are observable trends among suicides, however: More
older people kill themselves than younger ones. And more males
take their own lives than females, though more women make
attempts that don't end in death.[4]

Take a look at some people who *succeeded* in killing themselves.

Wanda was a forty-eight-year-old woman who lived in a
semirural suburb with her husband and two children. Her father
had treated her badly when she was young, and she frequently
retreated to her mother's protective presence and avoided her
father whenever possible.

During her adolescence she developed a strong aversion to sex
and was never able to get rid of these feelings. Wanda said she and
her husband had averaged one act of sexual intercourse a month

until their second child was born during the third year of their marriage. Then she decided she couldn't take it any more and insisted that her husband keep away from her bed.

Her husband became quite irritable with this arrangement and began to nag and criticize, but she remained silent and took his abuse. She told me she had never been able to express anger toward a man and often took out her frustrations on herself by beating her head with her fists or pounding her arms against a wall. She became quite depressed and finally tried to take her life by slashing her wrists, but her husband found her in time and rushed her to the hospital.

A few months after her release, the depression set in again. This time she took no chances on failing to accomplish her purpose. She took a chain saw her husband kept in the garage, turned it on, and severed her right arm. Before anyone discovered her, she bled to death.

Mark was a nineteen-year-old college freshman who had always felt strong pressure from his parents to be an achiever both in academic work and in extracurricular activities. He had been a class officer in a small high school, graduated with honors, and generally regarded himself as quite popular with girls.

When he entered college, all that changed. The competition for grades was tougher, and he was just one among many in a large university. No one thought enough of him to nominate him for student government offices, and he had difficulty in establishing new relationships with women.

Mark studied hard, but at the end of the freshman year he had a C average. His marks in premed science courses were far below what he thought he would need to get into medical school. He became more and more depressed, and to top it all off his old high-school girl friend, whom he had wanted to date again, told him she was engaged to another guy.

Feeling a total failure, Mark could see no future for himself. He couldn't think outside the framework his parents had established for him. Finally, he went to a subway station, watched two trains speed by, and then as the third one bore down on him, he threw himself on the track below.

Margaret was a sixty-eight-year-old woman whose mother—a

ninety-two-year-old invalid—had just died after suffering with a painful form of cancer for several years. Margaret herself had been operated on for cancer, but the doctors had pronounced her cured.

Her husband had died two years before, and with no close relatives, she faced the prospect of living alone for the rest of her years. "I just seem to get more and more tired. I'm going to end up just like my mother," she said to a nurse who had been assigned to take care of her during a clinic visit for a checkup. "I don't think there's much sense for me to live any longer."

The nurses paid little attention to her feelings of depression because Margaret didn't seem abnormally dissatisfied with her lot in life. Two days after her clinic visit, she took an overdose of barbiturates. She was found dead on the floor of her living room three days later.

Perhaps you find yourself wondering why anyone would want to kill himself when life is such a precious and scarce commodity. Our research and that of others over the past decade has shown that there's no single feature that applies to all cases of self-destruction. The motivations are almost as varied as each human personality. Some of the more common reasons are:

- Retaliation, or the wish to punish another by inducing guilt
- Reunion with someone who has already died
- Escape from an intolerable or hopeless situation
- Destruction of unbearable feelings or impulses
- Atonement for some wrong to reduce guilt feelings
- An inner need to show courage and conquest of fear of death
- A desire to be reborn, or reincarnated

It's always hard to determine why a person kills himself unless he leaves a note explaining his reasons. Dr. Edwin Shneidman, pioneer researcher into suicidal behavior, has studied the content of many suicide notes and found that most contain rational arguments, but often are based on false premises.[5]

For example, a person may write, "I've failed in business, I'm doomed to be sneered at, looked down on. Nobody could possibly love me, so there's no sense in my continuing to live." This argument makes sense if you accept the writer's basic assumption that nobody loves a failure. Of course each of us fails in *something* at one time or another, yet we know the capacity to love and be loved is still there. Love, in other words, doesn't necessarily depend on success in business. This suicide note may be logical, but it's based on a false premise.

To help you understand more clearly why some people might take their own lives, check off some situations below that might possibly drive you to kill yourself. Don't be afraid to do this— considering the possibility of death by your own hand won't necessarily cause it to happen. Young psychotherapists who begin working with depressed patients are often afraid to ask if the person is thinking about killing himself. They're afraid that asking such a question might put an idea into the patient's head and ultimately lead to suicide. Clinical experience doesn't bear this out. So go ahead and look at the following possible reasons for suicide. Which ones might apply to you? Are there others not included? If so, jot them down at the bottom of the list.

I would consider taking my life:

_____ if I had a terminal illness and was going to die anyway.

_____ if I became permanently paralyzed, unable to move any part of my body.

_____ if I got persistently bored with life.

_____ if no one loved me any more.

_____ if I could no longer work and support myself.

_____ if I had severe pain which couldn't be relieved.

_____ if I lost the person who is now closest to me in life.

_____ if I disgraced my family and myself.

_____ if I was about to go insane.

_____ if I really wanted to hurt someone badly by inducing guilt feelings in him through my death.

_____ Another reason (Specify): _____

_____

Since most people don't leave suicide notes, their motivations frequently have to be reconstructed after death through the use of a "psychological autopsy," a systematic effort to determine the context of a death by assessing the social and emotional events surrounding the death. In our research at Harvard, we have studied numerous suicides using the psychological autopsy approach and found two general themes or motivations that seem involved in many suicides. We call them *payback* and *escape*. Most suicides contain some degree of payback and escape in varying proportions.[6]

Payback simply means that a person kills himself to spite somebody he dislikes or somebody he thinks has wronged him. You may wonder, "How can killing yourself hurt anybody else?" But consider the tremendous guilt feelings which a suicide can cause in the survivor. A person who kills himself and leaves a note for his spouse saying, "You should have treated me better," implies something like this: "I'm dead, and it's all your fault, you louse. You did it. You should feel guilty, and I want you to feel guilty all of your life!"

Sometimes payback involves getting even with someone who is already dead. In other words, you may have an unhealthy identification with a dead person and feel that the deceased is somehow a part of you. You may kill yourself as a final measure to destroy this presence you feel. But unfortunately, you won't be around to enjoy the freedom you were looking for.

Freud reflects this notion in his early thinking on suicide: "Probably no one finds the mental energy required to kill himself, unless in the first place, in doing so he is at the same time killing an object [person] with whom he has identified himself, and in the second place, is turning against himself a death wish which has not been directed against someone else."[7]

The second common motivation we've found for suicides is called escape. Suppose you found yourself facing a tough situation which seemed to offer no way out. What would you do in such a case? You could opt for death. You may say, "No situation can be so difficult or inescapable that it can be changed only by death." Maybe so. But imagine the worst series of catastrophes that might happen to you: financial failure; loss of all your loved ones; bad health; public disgrace. Suppose, in other words, that you faced even worse disasters than those confronting the Old Testament figure, Job. You still might not consider suicide to be a viable alternative, but it would at least be an issue to contend with, wouldn't it?

The escape motivation is invariably accompanied by a condition called *delusional hopelessness.*[8] Some situations, by most objective standards, really are hopeless. But others may only seem hopeless. A person may only have a delusion, a false belief, that there is no out, no exit. Such delusions of no escape lead many people to suicide.

Take a fifty-four-year-old man I knew who had a successful business in a large eastern city. His business failed, and he ended his life by jumping off the top of a tall office building. He left behind his wife and three children.

From his standpoint there was no way out of his financial dilemma, no alternative except to die. But he failed to see how hopeful the situation looked to those with a more realistic perspective. From the vantage point of others, including his family, there was much that could still have been done. They could have sold their large home and moved to a smaller place. The wife and older children could have gotten jobs. But he thought that everything was hopeless and death was the only answer.

This delusional hopelessness often goes hand in hand with another psychological malady called *clinical depression.*[9] Most of us have "down" days when nothing goes right and we feel blue, lonely, and sad. These feelings are normal; a day or so later, things begin to look better and we get on an even mental keel again. But when a person's mood swings too low and stays there, he has become clinically depressed. In addition to a dejected mood, clinical depression may include physical manifestations such as loss of appetite, sleep disturbance, and the loss of interest in sex. When clinical depression sets in, suicide is always a possibility. In fact, depression is the one clinical symptom most frequently associated with suicide.

When delusional hopelessness and clinical depression combine like an unbearable lead weight on your shoulders, you may begin to believe that there's no hope. Any outsider may be able to see that your beliefs about your problems are unrealistic. But to you they're quite real. It's in this dark time of depression and hopelessness that many decisions to commit suicide are made.

One woman patient felt she had disgraced her family and friends by making an unsuccessful attempt on her own life. She was convinced that they would never forgive her and that for the rest of her life people would point at her and say, "There's the crazy woman who tried to kill herself." She escaped this fantasied possibility by successfully taking her own life.

Do you ever feel that you are in a situation where there's no escape? If you killed yourself, would it be to escape a bad situation, or would you more likely do it to pay back someone for doing you wrong? Take a minute to think about this.

As you thought about the possibility of killing yourself, the moral implications of suicide probably crossed your mind. Can suicide ever be a right choice? Rest assured you have a great deal of company in asking such a question. The right of a person to take his own life has been the object of discussion and debate since the earliest days of human ethics. Arguments have been heated and extensive on both sides of the issue.

The stoic philosopher Seneca said, "As I choose the ship in which I will sail and the house I will inhabit, so I will choose the death by which I leave life. It would be far better for one to choose death rather than to see the noble parts of him be eaten away by old age or disease."[10]

Another pro-suicide voice is A. E. Hotchner, who, writing about the suicide of Ernest Hemingway, said the author chose destruction rather than defeat. It's better for man to be destroyed but undefeated rather than attempt a compromise with the inevitability of time, Hotchner argued.[11]

The arguments against suicide are just as strong. Aristotle said, "to seek death in order to escape from poverty or the pangs of love, or from pain or sorrow, is not the act of a courageous man but rather of a coward, for it is weakness to fly from troubles, and suicide does not endure death because it is noble to do so but to escape evil."[12]

A forceful religious argument was offered in the third century by St. Augustine, who wrote in the *City of God* that suicide is never justified for the following reasons: 1) the Christian is never without hope as long as the possibility of repentance remains alive, but with suicide, the possibility of repentance is gone; 2) suicide is homicide, and this is a forbidden act; 3) if there is sin worthy of death, God is the judge and not the Christian; and 4) suicide is the greater sin than any other choice which might be the lesser sin.[13]

This controversy about a person's right to take his own life is still going on today. A debate was held recently in San Francisco with two mental health experts, Dr. Thomas Szasz and Dr. Edwin Shneidman, squaring off against each other.[14]

Dr. Szasz, a noted critic of prevailing American psychiatric views, took a strong pro-suicide position by arguing that each individual has a practically unlimited right to take his own life. Suicide, he said, does not presuppose a diseased state of mind, even though most psychiatrists look at it that way. And outside restraints on a person who has decided to kill himself are a violation of a person's personal liberties. Szasz also contended that unrequested psychiatric intervention is based on the outmoded idea that human life belongs to God and that only God can decide its tenure. We, in contrast, live in a secular age which can provide no such justification for suicide prevention.

Dr. Shneidman, who founded the first and most effective American suicide prevention center in Los Angeles, forcefully took the opposing side. While intervention by suicide workers may temporarily deny a person's freedom, he argued, preventing such self-destruction can result in an even greater freedom—the freedom from mental anguish.

He said that many people who are in the throes of despair aren't certain they want to kill themselves. As a result, they shouldn't be left to their own devices. Instead, we should restrain and give aid to those who are sad and depressed, especially if they display confusion or uncertainty about their intentions and cry out for help.

Shneidman also argued that survivors of a suicide have rights, including the right to an unstigmatized life. Szasz agrees, but adds that suicide is a social wrong which shames survivors simply because psychiatry has erroneously made suicide an abnormal act.

As this debate rages on, with physicians, psychologists, and theologians entering the verbal fray, I've come to several personal conclusions. Whether a person has a right to kill himself is not the essential issue. If a person is really convinced that he wants to kill himself, then the question of whether he has the right to act need never be considered. He simply does it, without giving anyone a chance to object. Suicide prevention is only for those who place themselves in a position to get help. The man who hangs from the top of a bridge until the police arrive or who calls a prevention center is voluntarily showing his ambivalence. His rights aren't being taken away from him without his consent because, through his actions, he was the first to indicate his desire for help.

Ultimately then, suicide is something you do by yourself. If you don't want help, you'll surely kill yourself eventually. A person has to make up his own mind about the ethics of his act, including the impact of his death on those he leaves behind. In the last analysis, it's a matter of individual morality. The ultimate decision can be influenced, but it can't be made by anyone else.

The fact that the decision to kill yourself finally rests with you makes it sound like suicide is a rational choice, but that isn't always the case because impulsive, unthinking emotions often enter in. Still, there is a very strong argument that suicide *should* be rational because it's irreversible. You don't get another chance if you make the wrong decision. In my clinical experience I've found that in a rational consideration of suicide, three factors seem to be significant:

1. **Cost to Survivors.**   I've worked with the survivors of suicide, and I question whether a person can ever get over the impact of such a death. Quite apart from the social stigma which Dr. Shneidman pointed out in his debate with Dr. Szasz, there are other profound psychological repercussions.

Some of my most interesting encounters with survivors of suicide involved several young men who were in their early teens—a very impressionable age for emotional development— when their fathers killed themselves. These young men were referred to me for treatment several years after their fathers died, because they were having emotional difficulties. In each case, the patient had the compelling, almost fatalistic sense that he was doomed to end up like his father, dying by his own hand.

In the loss of anyone close to you, there are a variety of feelings such as sadness, relief, and anger. Acknowledgment of these feelings is necessary for grief to be resolved. If someone close to you kills himself and leaves you alone, you may feel extremely angry and resentful. This anger can become so intense that it's almost impossible for you to express it and find relief. The intensity of the anger may cause you to turn your hostile feelings back on yourself and begin to experience strong guilt feelings.

Survivors of suicide often become obsessed with the idea that there just might have been something they could have done to prevent the death. Deaths by natural and even accidental causes can be grieved and forgotten, but a death by suicide is likely to linger and affect the rest of the survivor's life.

2. Ambivalence. There is a small voice in nearly every suicidal person that seems to keep whispering, "Stay alive!" Part of each of us wants to keep on living, no matter how depressed or frustrated with life we may become. This struggle between the affirmation and negation of life results in an ambivalence that's most clearly illustrated in the suicide attempt that fails.

I've noticed that even though the forces that drove them to try to kill themselves may not have changed, a number of patients who have made unsuccessful suicide attempts often express pleasure that they're still alive. One woman leaped from a tall bridge and through a fluke of circumstances managed to survive. When I visited her in the hospital, she told me that just as she had leaped and was plummeting down through the air, she had changed her mind. She wished she hadn't jumped.

It's impossible to tell whether those who *succeed* in killing themselves had the same degree of ambivalence because they're not around to describe their feelings. But my interviews with people like this woman, who could have been dead except for a quirk of fate, suggest that the attitudes of the successful suicides are probably not very different from those who fail.

This ambivalence—this feeling that you're not completely sure you want to die—warrants some careful second and third thoughts about entering into such an irreversible decision.

3. Hope. Even if a person is completely unambivalent, absolutely sure it's better to die than live with some oppressive problem, there is one final thing he should consider in making a rational suicide decision. I've already spoken of delusional hopelessness—the false belief that nothing can be done about some problem and that the only solution is death. If you are depressed, you may feel this way. But depressions, just like an oppressive fog or a violent thunderstorm, do lift. And things begin to look different when the black mood shifts to reveal a brighter horizon.

Circumstances that bothered you may not have altered, but to the person who is not depressed, things always look more manageable.

There is always hope that things will change for the better. The most important thing is time, and for many people, the right kind of medical intervention. The use of antidepressant drugs is beyond the scope of this chapter, but even these drugs, which are very effective, require time to work. How to buy time so that your hope can be revived—that's the issue.

The strong person can tell himself, "If I can just stick it out, things will look up when I'm not so depressed." For others, some form of hospitalization or surveillance is necessary to provide the necessary time for hope to appear.

Of course, there's always the possibility that circumstances may really be hopeless. But in most cases, there is some reasonable ground for hope, some chance that once the depression has departed, other courses of action will seem more reasonable than suicide.

There is some evidence that attitudes in the United States toward certain types of suicide may be changing. Michael Connell, Clinical Professor of Psychiatry at Tulane Medical School, surveyed a large number of physicians and college students about their views on suicide. He found that the younger people were more likely to be sympathetic than the older physicians toward a terminally ill person who takes his own life.[15] Dr. Shneidman, in a survey done for *Psychology Today*, found that sixty-eight percent of his 30,000 respondents conceded some justifiable circumstances for suicide and fifteen percent believed that society has no right to stop a person who wants to commit suicide.[16]

These surveys are easier to understand if we look at a few specific examples. Henry, a seventy-two-year-old man with an advanced terminal illness, was assigned to a private room in a hospital. Despite good care, he continued to go downhill and the doctors gave him about three days to live. At that point, though very weak and near death, he managed to drag himself over to the window in his room, open it, and jump to his death.

This is not an isolated example. Another terminally-ill man in a very feeble condition killed himself by stuffing his throat with tissue which he found on his bedstand. He suffocated to death.

Why should these men, so close to death, want to end their own lives? Why not just wait for nature to take its course?

The answers to these questions may be revealed in part through a look at Leo, a ninety-two-year-old man who worked as a superintendent in a small apartment building. He contracted a gangrenous foot infection. After suffering with it for a few weeks, he announced to two friends of mine who lived in his building, "I don't want my foot removed. I've lived long enough. It's time for me to die."

In their uneasiness, my friends tried to talk him into returning to the hospital for the surgery which he needed. But he steadfastly refused. They sensed something ominous in his statement, "I want to die," but didn't know quite what to do.

Leo had only one relative, a niece from whom he was estranged, and he wanted to be sure that she got none of his small estate. He asked my friends if they would get him a lawyer so he could be sure his things would be disposed of as he wished. They found him a lawyer.

On the same day that he signed his will, Leo shot himself. My friends found him after they returned home from a movie.

Interviews with those who knew Leo revealed that he felt he couldn't sustain the pain from his foot, nor could he stand the thought of having others assist him in and out of bed as he got worse. He had been offered medical treatment and hospitalization, but had refused both because he felt they would only postpone his inevitable physical degeneration.

Leo is an example of a man who wanted to be self-determined, completely in control of his destiny with the right to end his life. He wanted to decide how much pain to bear and the limits of the indignity he would endure. The other two elderly people—Henry, who jumped to his death, and the man who swallowed the tissue—may have fallen into the same category. What kind of a personal reaction do you have to the actions of these three men?

Check one or more of the following:

_____ They were wrong and God will punish them.
_____ I can understand how they must have felt.
_____ I am repelled and would never do the same.
_____ Under the circumstances, I might do the same.

_____ They leave me with a very mixed feeling.

_____ I don't have any reaction that I'm aware of.

_____ Other (Specify: _____)

Before you make a final judgment about your own attitudes toward suicide, let me share with you one final example which I found personally moving and disturbing.

Ken was a forty-eight-year-old man in our hospital suffering with the type of terminal cancer which produces an unbearable amount of pain. Because he asked the nurse to give him something to end his life and put an end to the pain, I was called into the case.

In order to control the intractable pain, he was treated with a type of brain surgery in which parts of the brain associated with pain were severed. This managed to control the pain problem but radically changed his behavior. Before he died, his behavior became quite animal-like. He was frequently found swinging on the furniture, exposing himself and engaging in other bizarre behavior in front of his wife and small children. If I had the choice between unbearable pain, an undignified death before my family, or the chance to end my life by being given some pill which would cause a quiet death, I must confess that I would be hard pressed not to choose the latter.

Suicide is the most drastic method of affecting your life span and coping with life's stresses. Even if you don't opt for suicide, setting up a theoretical alternative of self-destruction can give you a sense of perspective—a sense that the difficulty you're facing won't make any difference a few years from now, after you're dead. Also, with the ultimate way out clearly before you, you are free to explore other less drastic alternatives to the problems of life.

1. Friedrich Wilhelm Nietzsche, "Beyond Good and Evil."
2. Rollo May, *Existence* (New York: Basic Books, 1958), 90.
3. Rudolph Reitler, in *On Suicide*, P. Freidman (ed) (New York: IUP, 1967).
4. N.L. Farberow and Edwin S. Shneidman, *Cry for Help* (New York: McGraw Hill, 1957).
5. Edwin S. Shneidman and N.L. Farberow, *Clues to Suicide* (New York: McGraw Hill, 1957).

6. Data from this research can be found in:
Avery D. Weisman and J. William Worden, "Risk-Rescue Rating in Suicide Assessment." Arch. Gen. Psychiatry, 26: (June, 1972), 553-560.
J. William Worden and Robert S. Sterling-Smith, "Lethality Patterns in Multiple Suicide Attempts." *Life-Threatening Behavior,* 3(1973), 95-104.
Avery D. Weisman, *The Realization of Death: A Guide for the Psychological Autopsy* (New York: Jason Aronson, 1974).
J. William Worden, "Lethality Factors and the Suicide Attempt." in Edwin S. Shneidman, *Suicidology: Contemporary Developments* (New York: Grune and Stratton, 1976).
7. Sigmund Freud, "The Psychogenesis of a Case of Homosexuality in a Woman." (1920)
8. J. Fawcett, M. Less, and W.E. Bunney Jr., "Suicide. Clues from Interpersonal Communication." *Arch. Gen. Psychiatry,* 21:(Aug., 1969), 129-137.
9. For a basic introduction to the subject of clinical depression, see:
D. Schuyler, *The Depressive Spectrum* (New York: Jason Aronson, 1974).
10. H.R. Fedden, *Suicide, A Social and Historical Study* (London: Peter Davies, 1938).
11. A.E. Hotchner, *Papa Hemingway* (New York: Random House, 1966).
12. Aristotle: *Nicomachen Ethics.*
13. St. Augustine: *City of God,* M. Dods (trans.) (New York: The Modern Library, 1950).
14. "Suicide Prevention: Myth or Mandate?" A debate sponsored by the University of California and the Suicide Prevention Center of San Mateo County.
15. Michael L. Connell, "Suicide—Right or Privilege? Attitudes of Two Populations." Unpublished manuscript.
16. Edwin S. Shneidman, "You and Death." *Psychology Today,* (June, 1971), 79.

V

Free at Last

Muriel Vos

Chapter Fourteen

GLIMPSES OF THE OTHER SIDE

Since prehistoric times, men have been fascinated by the question of what lies beyond this life. Is there an ultimate freedom on the other side of death, or the final bondage of nothingness? The only hints of an answer come from a small number of people who have tasted death and lived to tell about it.

One of the best-known ancient accounts of a person returning from the dead is the biblical story of Lazarus, the brother of Mary and Martha and the friend of Jesus. The Gospel of John doesn't tell us what Lazarus saw or experienced during the several days that he was dead, but the philosopher L. N. Andrieve has captured the spirit of curiosity that must have gripped the bystanders when they saw Lazarus walking out of his tomb at Jesus' command.

"Why dost thou not tell us what happened in the beyond?" the observing neighbors and relatives might have asked, but Lazarus remained silent.

"For three days had he been dead," Andrieve writes. "Thrice had the sun risen and set, but he had been dead; children had played, streams had murmured over pebbles, the wayfarer had stirred up the hot dust in the highroad . . . but he had been dead. And now he was again among them; he touched them, he looked at them . . . looked at them! And through the black discs of his pupils, as through darkened glass, stared the unknowable beyond."

In recent times, a number of people like Lazarus have been declared clinically dead but have returned to life again. Advances in medical technology have made it easier to revive people who are on the verge—or over the edge—of death. Lazarus' lips remained sealed, but many others have chosen to talk about the "unknowable beyond," and they have given us a great deal to consider about our own deaths.

When I was a teenager, our minister announced one Sunday morning that a highly unusual man would speak to us at the church the following Wednesday evening. He was billed as a person who had been medically dead for a brief period and then revived in a hospital. Hearing such a story intrigued me, so I, with several hundred others, crowded into our church basement and waited expectantly for this adventurer who had looked his own death in the face and had lived to tell about it.

Even now I can recall him—an ordinary-looking man who did not seem the type of person to brave such a perilous encounter. But as he started speaking, I tried to put myself in his shoes and experience what he had been through. I can remember only a few fragments of what he said: "I had the sense of peace . . . a feeling I was slipping away . . . suspended by some force outside myself . . . perhaps God."

It was all very interesting, but much too abbreviated to satisfy me completely. As I left church that evening, I felt a little more hopeful about my own death, a little more informed about what I could expect. But like most others who have heard these accounts of the other side, I wanted to know more. Of course until we die ourselves we can never know exactly what death feels like or what it involves. Still, it's possible to get some immediate sense of the experience if we listen closely to the stories of a number of people who have, in effect, "died" and come back to life.

Carl Jung, one of Freud's disciples, wrote in his autobiography about a time when he "hung on the edge of death" after a heart attack.[1] At one point during that crisis, he felt himself floating away from earth, which he pictured as being a thousand miles away, bathed in a glorious blue light.

Then the scene around him changed so that he was standing before a temple, the door of which was surrounded by a wreath of flames. "As I approached . . . I had the feeling that everything was being sloughed away," Jung wrote. "Everything I aimed at or wished for or thought, the whole phantasmagoria of earthly existence fell away or was stripped from me—an extremely painful process."

As he approached the temple, Jung said, he believed he would enter an "illuminated room" where he could meet those people who had been most meaningful to him during his life. He would also gain an insight into the "historical nexus [that] I, or my life, fitted into."

Then the setting shifted again and the psychoanalyst found

himself in a beautiful and peaceful garden of pomegranates. "It is impossible to convey the beauty and intensity of emotion during these visions," he recalled. "They were the most tremendous things I have ever experienced. . . . I can describe the experience only as the ecstasy of a nontemporal state in which present, past, and future are one. Everything that happens in time had been brought together into a concrete whole. . . . One is interwoven into an indescribable whole and yet observed it with complete objectivity."

A similar kind of enchantment with death enveloped Caresse Crosby, who in her autobiography *The Passionate Years,* described how she narrowly escaped drowning at the age of seven.[2] "When my head plunged beneath the water's surface, I took one long frightened gulp and I never got another breath of air," she said. "My lungs expelled once and refilled with tide water. The blood rushed from my toes to my nose and suddenly my head seemed to expand and explode, but softly as though it were a cotton ball fluffing out and out and out."

She soon began to hear "strange sea lullabies," and then a bright flash of insight cleared her mind so that she could see and understand everything around her. She saw her father at work on his boat, oblivious to the frantic, frightened efforts of her brothers to rescue her. The father finally turned and rushed over to her limp body, and she watched the frenzied efforts to revive her.

But Crosby sensed that she was almost happy with her drowning condition. "I tried not to come back," she remembered. "It was the most perfect state of easeful joy that I ever experienced, then or since. There was no sadness or sickness from which I wished to escape. I was only seven, a carefree child, yet that moment in all my life has never been equaled for pure happiness. Could I have glimpsed, while drowned (for I was drowned), the freedom of eternal life? One thing I know, that Nirvana does exist between here and the hereafter—a space of delight, for I have been there."

Many people who have had a close brush with death at first feel themselves struggling fearfully against the ebbing away of their lives. But then they begin to accept and even enjoy moving into the realm of the dead. A psychoanalyst, Dr. Robin Hunter, reported a case involving a nurse who needed some antibiotic, but didn't know whether she was allergic to penicillin.[3] As she and her husband were driving down a highway, she popped a pill into her mouth. When her breathing started becoming more difficult, she immediately realized her mistake. "Frantic fear" gripped her, but this feeling soon passed, and in retrospect she decided she would never fear dying again.

"But I felt an intense sympathy for my husband," she said. "Then I felt guilty that I was putting him through this ordeal. I was ashamed. I remember a last violent reaction in which I fought desperately ... but I was not afraid and then I gave in, knowing I wanted death."

The nurse's attention became riveted on a series of quick scenes from her former life, which flashed in rapid succession as though with a brilliant strobe light. Vivid colors rushed into her vision: a favorite doll which seemed to have developed extremely bright blue glass eyes ... an image of herself as a child riding on a fire engine-red bicycle across a glistening green lawn. Though each of these scenes was different, they were tied together by an "ecstatically happy feeling." She then moved into a state of "bliss and ecstasy," and found herself contemplating a beautiful image of the Taj Mahal.

This woman, in a mood reminiscent of Caresse Crosby, resisted being pulled back into the world of the living. As she became aware of people trying to wake her up, she felt "resentful and irritated. I wanted to be left alone with the beautiful dream of the Taj Mahal. Then I became aware of an oxygen mask, and the fact that an intravenous was running. I reluctantly regained consciousness to find myself in the emergency O.P.D. of a hospital."

Not all such encounters with death have been quite so positive, however. In a study conducted by Russell Noyes, Jr., and LeRoy Kletti, a couple of persons found themselves "lost in hell."[4] One woman nearly drowned when she was fourteen years old. As she went under the water for what she thought was the final time before death, she saw "my whole life, from the time I was a small child to the age of fourteen, [appear] before me as though on a screen. ... I was so very sorry for the things I had done but felt it was too late. Spiritually I was lost. God would judge me doomed and unfit for heaven."[5]

Despite exceptions like this, many people who have come close to death have had positive feelings which often surpassed any happiness they have known in life. How do you interpret this? Do you find it strange that sometimes these people didn't even want to return to life?

One fascinating experience accompanying many near-death incidents is the victim's sense that his spirit or conscious personality has been detached from his body. When Captain Roy Huffine,[6] a commercial airline pilot, first learned to fly, he decided to take a spin in a small airplane one day with his wife, Roselyn. He revved up the engines and started rolling faster and faster down the runway. But just as he pulled back on the stick, something went wrong. The plane failed to lift far enough off the ground, careened off the end of the runway and piled up in a smoking heap off the field. Huffine, who was thrown clear and received a severe blow to the head, suddenly sensed that he, or at least his conscious personality, was no longer in the wreckage.

"I was . . . observing the whole scene from about fifty feet away from the plane," he recalled. "I saw Roselyn struggling to unfasten the safety belt which still held her. Hot vapor burst from the engine. At last Roselyn rolled free onto the ground."

Another form lay on the ground beside her, and he soon realized it was his own body, "but it did not contain the consciousness with which I was observing all that was happening. Roselyn was dragging the body away from the smoking plane. I watched with indifference."

As the drama unfolded before him, Huffine felt no pain, but "only a feeling of completeness and well-being." Cars began arriving on the airfield and soon spectators were walking around the wreckage and talking excitedly. Huffine could hear everything these people were saying, and some of the comments were not particularly complimentary about him.

"Well, he must have been a wild one!" one woman said to her male companion as she looked at Huffine's body. "It's no more than he deserved! Only birds are supposed to fly!"

Then one of the pilot's friends, a man named Ed, rushed up to the plane and pulled Roselyn aside. "Is he dead?" Ed asked.

"I don't know, " she replied, crying.

Ed bent over and felt Huffine's pulse. "Somebody hurry! Get an ambulance!" he cried. He began to apply artificial respiration, but the lifeless form failed to respond. Finally, Ed grabbed his friend's shoulders in frustration, shook his body and shouted, "Roy! Roy! Can you hear me?"

At this urgent crying of his name, Huffine, who had been watching all this activity from outside his body, "felt as if a strong wire were tugging me back toward my body. I was reluctant to return and continued to look, experiencing the most complete contentment."

But Ed was insistent and he continued to call the pilot's name. The pull became stronger and stronger until Huffine finally realized he was no longer outside his own body, but was inside, looking up at his friend's and wife's faces.

"Oh, my God, Roy, we thought you were gone!" Ed cried. Roselyn gripped her husband's hand and was unable to control the tears that were rushing down her cheeks. Ed helped Roy struggle to his feet, but before they walked away, Roy knew there was something he had to do. As he passed the couple he had heard talking about him, he leaned over and told the woman, "I heard what you said about me."

The woman looked shocked because she and her male companion had been watching the events too far away to have been heard, even by someone who wasn't injured. "I didn't say anything," she protested. But when Huffine repeated what he had heard, the woman turned white and ran off to her car.

A particularly upsetting example of this kind of detached spirit or consciousness at death involved a fifty-year-old woman who was in a hospital suffering from internal bleeding.[7] She could feel herself becoming weaker and weaker. She sensed her chances to live were quite slim when a nurse entered the room and immediately ran to find a resuscitation team.

As the medical staff worked over her, the patient knew precisely who was in the room, but she herself "seemed to be floating a few feet above, watching the procedure. I was aware of only one feeling in myself—to tell those working on me to let go and not to be upset.... I then floated away, unaware that the team gave up in their efforts to revive me."

The woman returned to consciousness inside her own body as a hospital orderly was pushing her toward the morgue. She pulled the bed sheet off her own face, and the shocked orderly immediately changed his plans about filing her as a cadaver. Apparently embarrassed by their mistake, the hospital staff seemed uninterested in talking with her about the incident. When she was well enough to be released from the hospital, they discharged her without any further discussion of the matter. She eventually wanted to reassure herself of her own sanity, so she sought help from Dr. Elisabeth Kubler-Ross, who told the woman she was perfectly normal and need not worry.

One of the most detailed accounts of this disembodied state of death came from a sixty-eight-year-old Canadian man who suffered a severe cardiac arrest. According to a report published in the *Journal of the Canadian Medical Association*,[8] the man said, "I saw myself leave my body, coming out through my head and shoulders. . . . The 'body' leaving me was not exactly in vapour form, yet it seemed to expand very slightly once it was clear of me. It was somewhat transparent, for I could see my other 'body' through it."

As the man felt his consciousness become separated from his physical body, he thought, "So this is what happens when you die."

Then suddenly the separation of body and spirit was complete, and he found himself sitting on a small object that was bearing him up at a blinding speed into a dull, blue-gray sky. "It's lonely out here," he thought. "Where am I going to end up? This is one journey I must take alone."

As he soared up at a forty-five degree angle, he looked down and saw a "pure white cloud-like substance . . . perfectly rectangular in shape . . . but full of holes" which was also moving up on a line that would intersect his own path.

"What will happen to me when it engulfs me?" he asked himself.

Then another thought seemed immediately to answer his question: "You don't have to worry. It has all happened before and everything will be taken care of."

But the collision never took place, and the next thing that happened to the man on his fantastic journey was a "sensation of

floating in a bright, pale yellow light—a very delightful feeling."
Although he was not conscious of having any lower limbs, he felt
something being torn off a set of scars on his right leg, as if a
large piece of adhesive tape had been taken off.

"They have always said your body is made whole out here," he
mused. "I wonder if my scars are gone?"

He couldn't locate his legs, however, and he continued to float
around, "enjoying the most beautiful tranquil sensation. I had
never experienced such a delightful sensation and have no words
to describe it." This sense of peace and happiness was soon
interrupted by "sledgehammer blows" on his left side, in the
vicinity of his heart. Though he felt no pain, he had difficulty
maintaining his balance on the object where he was perched. He
began to count the blows as they pounded against him, and when
he reached six, he said, "What the hell are you doing to me?"

He then opened his eyes, realized he was in control of all his
physical faculties, and immediately recognized the doctors and
nurses around him.

Similar feelings and visions during close brushes with death have
been reported by a number of other people. The highly dramatic
and even mystical quality of these spiritual adventures has probably provoked some reaction in you, so take a moment to examine
your present awareness and note it below:

____ These stories are too weird. They turn me off.

____ I want to think more about it.

____ These accounts give me an optimistic feeling about my
own death.

____ I know someone who went through something similar.

____ Some of these incidents confirm what I've always be-
lieved about death.

____ None of these accounts had anything to do with reality.
These people were merely delusional: Their minds were
playing tricks on them.

____ I want to think about something else because
_____ .

____ Other: _____ .

Some psychologists may argue that the blissful feelings and
sense of separation of body and spirit at death merely represent

the brain's way of helping an individual cope with the threat of nonexistence. Theologians, on the other hand, may say the experiences indicate the entry of the human spirit into another realm of existence. There will probably also be disagreement among those with a religious orientation. Some will contend that the generally happy orientation of those who looked death in the face confirms the idea that there is no hell, and that most, if not all of us are destined for some sort of harmony with God in heaven. Others—especially traditional Christians who believe that only a few are destined for eternal life with God—will counter that the expressions of happiness are appropriate only because these people have not yet had their lives evaluated at the Last Judgment.

Regardless of which of these interpretations appeals to you, there seem to be at least three phases that some of us may go through as our last spark of life flickers out. Russell Noyes, a psychiatrist who has been one of the major investigators into this phenomenon, has labeled these phases resistance, life review, and transcendence.[9]

Resistance occurs when you recognize that your death is imminent. You get anxious and panicky, and an increased alertness enhances your physical and mental abilities. At the same time this lifesaving energy is swelling up inside you, however, the seeds are being sown for an equally strong urge to surrender to death. Gradually, this urge to surrender surpasses the will to live, and then fear subsides and inner tranquility sets in.[10]

The *review* stage follows resistance. "As fear is replaced by calm and as active mastery is replaced by passive surrender, a curious splitting of the self from its bodily representation may occur," Noyes explains. At this point, you sense that you're stepping outside of your body and watching the surrounding events with detached interest. "The threat of death that you face is reduced to a threat of *bodily* annihilation."[11] The *real* you—your spirit or conscious personality—has become an observer of the physical danger to your body.

This review stage may also involve a review of past experiences, which are usually remembered with pleasure. You may seem to be rushing into the past or the past will be rushing by you. Noyes suggests that these flashbacks may result from your loss of future time orientation. When confronted with the end of your life, the past suddenly becomes overwhelmingly important.

The third and last stage is a sense of *transcendence.* You begin to regard yourself as a different sort of being and may feel as though you're "outside of time in eternity, or beyond the past or the future." Noyes says, "The experience . . . represents complete immersion in the present moment, a phenomenon accompanied by an altered sense of time."[12]

In addition to the sense of transcending time, you also feel yourself moving above and outside physical space and individual identity. You experience a oneness with other human beings and with the universe and may be struck with some insight about ultimate truth, some understanding about the universe and your precise place in it. The state of transcendence and immersion into other forms of reality may also be accompanied by a feeling of passive surrender and pervasive calmness or ecstasy.[13]

Most of the examples we've looked at involved people in a relatively good state of health who were suddenly threatened with death. The most important factor in triggering these different stages of awareness seems to have been the personal conviction that the person was close to death. Those with a chronic terminal illness may also pass through similar stages and reach a type of mystical and transcendent state when they become aware of the certainty of their death. Terminally ill patients who consistently deny death, however, may never be free enough to experience this expanded consciousness.

There appears to be some hope about our last earthly experience, whether we conclude that these visions of transcendence are mere fantasy or actual glimpses of another world that awaits us. After we recognize that all is lost and completely let go of our tight grip on life, inner peace and contentment seem possible during those last moments. Dying and death can never be the most pleasant or desirable experience and I would not want to see us over-romanticize it. Our mortality becomes a discomforting part of our lives the day we are born, and remains a conscious or subconscious adversary, ever growing in power, until our appointed time finally arrives. Death suggests not only terror and annihilation, however; it also offers possibility and choice through optimal Personal Death Awareness. If we unmask some of the mysteries surrounding death and dying—if we shine a light of understanding into the abyss—we *can* break free of denial and fear. We can replace confusion with meaning, and helplessness with power.

1. Carl G. Jung, *Memories, Dreams, Reflections* (New York: Random House, Inc., 1961).
2. Caresse Crosby, *The Passionate Years* (New York: The Dial Press, 1953).
3. Robin C. A. Hunter, "On the Experience of Nearly Dying," *Amer. J. Psychiatry,* 124(1967), 84-88.
4. Russell Noyes, Jr., and LeRoy Kletti, "Depersonalization in the Face of Life-Threatening Danger: An Interpretation," manuscript, 14.
5. Ibid., 12.
6. E. L. Huffine, "I Watched Myself Die," *Guideposts Magazine,* (May, 1964). Also reproduced in *The Vestibule,* ed. J. E. Weiss (Port Washington, New York: Ashley Books, Inc., 1972).
7. Elisabeth Kubler-Ross, "The Experience of Death," in *The Vestibule,* ed. J. E. Weiss (Port Washington, New York: Ashley Books, Inc., 1972).
8. R. L. MacMillan and K. W. G. Brown, "Cardiac Arrest Remembered," *C. M. A. Journal,* 104(1971), 889-890. Also in *The Vestibule,* J. E. Weiss, ed. (Port Washington, New York: Ashley Books, Inc., 1972).
9. Russell Noyes, "The Experience of Dying," *Psychiatry,* 35 (May, 1972), 174-184.
10. Ibid., 177.
11. Ibid., 178.
12. Ibid., 180.
13. Ibid., 180.

INDEX

191